The Diary of
Sarah Clin~

A Spirited Socialite
in Victorian Nova Scotia

Edited by
Meghan Hallett

Nimbus Publishing Limited
PO Box 9166
Halifax, NS   B3K 5M8
(902) 455-4286
Printed and bound in Canada
Designer: Kathy Kaulbach, Paragon Design Group

Front cover: "Four Ladies in Evening Dress," Emma Haliburton, 1840-1846. The ladies in this image are likely Haliburton's sisters at a social event. The Haliburton sisters, while older than Sarah, were known to her and they attended many of the same functions.
Title page: "View of Halifax," unknown artist, ca. 1850. This view of Halifax is much the same as the one that would have greeted Sarah upon her arrival in 1853.
Back cover photo: Johanna Smith

National Library of Canada Cataloguing in Publication Data

Clinch, Sarah
    The diary of Sarah Clinch : a spirited socialite in Victorian Nova Scotia
Includes bibliographical references and index.
ISBN 1-55109-376-6

1. Clinch, Sarah—Diaries. 2. Nova Scotia—Social life and customs—19th
    century. 3. Nova Scotia—History—1784-1867. 4. Socialites—Nova
    Scotia—Diaries. 5. Socialites—Massachusetts Boston—Diaries. I.
    Hallett, Meghan P., 1972- II. Title.

FC2322.1.C55A3 2001   971.6'02'092   C2001-902733-8
F1038.C58A3 2001

We acknowledge the financial support of the Government of Canada through the Book Publishing Industry Development Program (BPIDP) and the Canada Council for our publishing activities.

Acknowledgements

The research for this book has been nothing but an exercise in personal enjoyment. Following the twists and turns of Nova Scotia's history has only strengthened my belief that the world is a very small place. I would like to thank all of the people who have helped me—all of the staff at Nova Scotia Archives and Records Management, especially Lois Yorke; Tinker McKay, St. Paul's Church Archives; Christine Lovelace and Pat Townsend, Acadia University Archives; Anita Price, Dartmouth Heritage Museum; the staff of the Harvard University Archives; the New England Historic Genealogy Society; the Massachusetts Historical Society; Dr. Ron MacDonald, Army Museum, Citadel Hill; Lorraine Slopek, Anglican Diocesan Archives; Eva Major-Maorthy, National Archives of Canada; Ted Bond and Dale Clifton, Bond family genealogists; Laura Bradley, Yarmouth County Museum and Archives; Stephen P. Hall, Archivist, Beverly Historical Society and Museum; Peter O'Brien, Dalhousie University; my mother for helping me edit the diary in its early stages; and my family and friends for encouraging me to pursue this project. It is my hope that Sarah's journal not only provides an interesting and touching look into a young woman's life, but also brings to light some of the lesser-known history of this province and its people.

*This book is dedicated
to those who record their thoughts
and feelings in journals
and to Sarah,
who has become a friend
though we have never met.*

Table of Contents

Preface

I first met Sarah Apthorp Cunningham Clinch by chance five years ago. In search of a historical-based research topic, I went looking at the provincial archives. Not sure where to begin, I headed for the card catalogue and a drawer marked "diaries." I opened the drawer and began thumbing through the cards. Suddenly my research topic leaped out at me—"Sarah Clinch, young woman in Halifax, 1853-1854." I filled out a request slip and a member of the reference staff presented me with two small journals.

Immediately upon reading the diary, Sarah, mid-century Halifax, and mid-century Nova Scotia came alive. This young woman of eighteen had come to Nova Scotia from Boston to spend a year with her extended family. I felt a growing affinity with her as I read—the places that Sarah visits during her stay are the same places that I like to visit. I take regular walks in Point Pleasant Park, just like Sarah and her friends. I lived on South Street, the same street where Sarah resided during her time in Halifax. I have always enjoyed visiting St. Paul's Church, and I learned that Sarah's uncle was its curate. As a child my mother took me strawberry picking in Port Williams, usually followed by a picnic on the lawn at Prescott House. The Prescotts were Clinch family friends— Sarah even toured the gardens with Mr. Charles Ramage Prescott. My parents had indulged my childhood love of history and many family vacations were spent touring museums and provincial parks. These places were Sarah's Nova Scotia. The characters she met were familiar to me either from my childhood or from my studies. By simply walking the streets of Halifax I could imagine her five steps ahead; I only had to shut my eyes, and her words came alive.

I began by transcribing the journals, no easy task; although good, Sarah's handwriting was occasionally indecipherable. Once I had a functional copy, I began working to bring Sarah to life. I did what I could to learn as much as possible about her, but the more I learned, the more I realized how much her diary reflected the history of Nova Scotia. Entries referred to people with names like Uniacke, Haliburton, Allison, and Almon, and places like Government House, Citadel Hill, and Admiralty House. After five or six months of research, I was content with what I had completed—a transcribed version of the diary, a basic family history, and an overview of Halifax and Nova Scotia at mid-century—so I set the project aside for a while.

While I worked on my research, friends and family enjoyed hearing stories of Sarah and thought her diary very interesting. They encouraged me to "do something" with such a treasure. I did not think much about Sarah's diary until I re-read it five years later. Sarah pulled me into her world all over again, and my interest in her life and travels was renewed. There were people and places that I needed to identify and images of Sarah's friends and family that I wanted to locate. This new round of research differed in two ways: I had been employed in archival work for three years, and the role of the internet, particularly as a tool for searching out Sarah's American descendants, enhanced my archival research. Accession records at the provincial archives revealed that Sarah's journals had been donated in the 1960s by a relative who lived in a Boston suburb. Unfortunately, this relative passed away some years ago, so I was never able to learn how he came to possess the journals, nor could I benefit from his insight into her life. Luckily, he did recognize the contribution that her journals could make to Nova Scotians and he donated them to the province's archives. On the internet, amazingly, I found several very keen genealogists who kindly provided me with valuable information about the Bond family. The internet also allowed me to conduct research at archives in Boston and Cambridge. On-line finding aids and e-mail communications quickly started filling in the gaps of Sarah's life in Boston.

The journals themselves are contained in two small notebooks, which remain in excellent condition, almost as if Sarah had just finished writing in them. Their contents reveal not only a delightful look into Halifax and Nova Scotia in the 1850s, but also precious insight into the life of a wonderful young woman on the verge of adulthood. Shopping, visiting, and attending parties were part of Sarah's everyday life to be sure, but so were studying and prayer. Was Sarah aware of the ironies of her position in society as an upper-class woman—educated, but with no real recourse for her intellectual energies? At times, she appears to want only what her class and gender expect from her, for example to be content with not seeing the Lady Le Marchant but simply writing her name upon that lady's books (5 December 1853). At other times, however, Sarah's right to an education confronts her, for example in her encounter with "R. Haliburton [Robert, son of Thomas Chandler Haliburton], who thought fit to sneer at a girl knowing Latin" (29 June 1854). Educated in literature, world history, languages, and probably some mathematics and science, Sarah was taught to be creative and productive, yet as a Victorian woman of privilege she was denied the opportunity, such as I have in this project, to apply her knowledge and to express herself intellectually. I feel certain that Sarah would appreciate the further irony of my wanting to study her life and share it with others. I work in a field that I enjoy, compared to Sarah, whose greatest accomplishment, according to her society, would have been to marry well and have a family.

Society's constraints did have their effects on Sarah, but as the reader gets to know her, they see a young woman, class notwithstanding, who could be clumsy and awkward but who was not afraid to laugh at herself: "I threw the baby's coral hitch-ups into the fire this evening, mistaking them for apple parings in the low light. It was stupid enough to be sure, but that is nothing uncommon" (13 October 1853). A typical teenager, Sarah could also be moody and self-centered, greatly concerned with her appearance and social schedule.

The contents of the diaries have been transcribed word for word; occasional spelling and grammatical corrections have been made, but only when they improve readability. In several instances it is difficult to surmise whom Sarah is referring to, as she often misspells names. Throughout the diary she refers to various members of the Halliburton family. In mid-nineteenth-century Nova Scotia there were two prominent families with this last name, but with different spellings: "Haliburton" for Judge Thomas Chandler Haliburton and his family, and "Halliburton" for Chief Justice Brenton Halliburton and his relations. Sarah consistently used the latter spelling, making it impossible to identify which Halliburton or Haliburton she meant. As a sign of respect, Sarah used "Mr" and "Mrs" in place of first names when referring to others, a practice that also makes identification difficult.

S. Clinch.
Halifax,
N.S.
1854.

Time has allowed me only to scrape the surface of Sarah's life. Her friends and family were so deeply connected with the social history of Nova Scotia that one could trace them for years. When available, images that highlight some of the people and places in Sarah's life have been included. The most significant image missing is that of Sarah herself.

From New England to Nova Scotia

1837, the year eighteen-year-old Victoria was crowned queen of the British Empire, marks the beginning of one of the greatest eras of change that the world has seen. It was the age of Charles Dickens and Charles Darwin. Social reform, the rise of the middle class, advancements in science and industrialization, and British imperialism highlight the period. It was also the age of great wars. The Crimean War, the American Civil War, the Boer War, and the American-Mexican War shaped the lives of North Americans and citizens of the British Empire across the globe. Under Queen Victoria, the British Empire became one of the largest and most powerful nations of the nineteenth-century world, busy maintaining control over its colonial territories around the world, including those in North America.

The British Empire's control over its North American colonies was not always secure. In the seventeenth century, the British and the French struggled for domination of the lucrative fishing and fur-trading industries, and both raced to establish colonies. New France was in the process of falling to the British in the mid-eighteenth century, and the British looked to colonization as a way of solidifying their presence. This led to the expulsion of French-speaking Acadians from what are today the Maritime provinces of Canada. British officials invited loyal, English-speaking subjects from New England, now known as Planters, to re-settle the lands left vacant by the expulsion.

The Maritimes were again hit by a wave of American migration during the American War of Independence, which tried British control of North America. Many American residents who were loyal to the British king chose to leave their New England homes and move to the Maritimes. These Planter and Loyalist migrants were mostly English-speaking Protestants who were often born on American soil. The combination of American and British traditions brought to Nova Scotia by these colonists helped to shape the culture of eighteenth-century Nova Scotia. Immigration from Britain continued in the latter half of the eighteenth and in the early nineteenth centuries, giving turn-of-the-century Nova Scotia a decidedly British tone, despite the presence of other nationalities such as the Foreign Protestants from Germany. These founding ties remained a constant in nineteenth-century Nova Scotia and New England, secured by the presence of families and friends on both sides of the border.

Sarah Apthorp Cunningham Clinch lived and moved between these two worlds. She was born in Nova Scotia, as were her parents, but raised in Boston, the heart of revolutionary America only a century earlier. Although she had lived in "Yankeeland" all of her life, Sarah nevertheless identified with her British ancestry. She celebrated the Queen's birthday and, under her mother's firm guidance, did not adopt an American accent. Her father, trained in the Church of England, was an Episcopalian minister. Clearly, the Clinch family strove to uphold their British roots; maintaining close ties with their Nova Scotian relatives might have been one way for them to do so.

Sarah's Family Tree

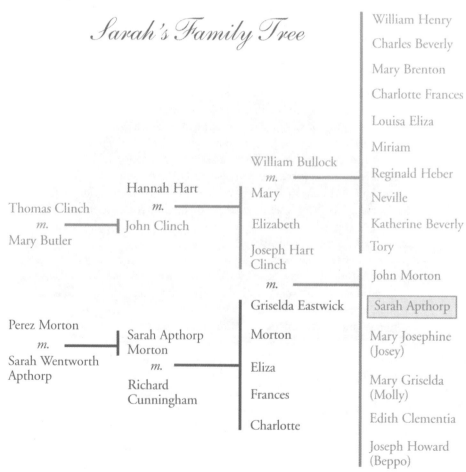

Life
in
Boston

Sarah Clinch was eighteen years old (the same age Victoria was when she took the British throne) when she began writing in her journal in the fall of 1853. An upcoming year-long trip to Nova Scotia prompted her to start recording her life's events.

The daughter of Griselda Eastwick Cunningham and Reverend Joseph Hart Clinch, Sarah was born on March 22, 1835 in Windsor, Nova Scotia. Joseph Clinch was the son of Dr. John Clinch, born circa 1806 in Trinity Bay, Newfoundland. Educated in part at King's Academy in Windsor, Sarah's father had such distinguished classmates as the Reverend William Bullock, Bishop Hibbert Binney, Judge Lewis Wilkins Jr., Judge Thomas Chandler Haliburton, and the Reverend George McCawley. Joseph Clinch was ordained by Bishop John Inglis, spent some time in Wilmot, Nova Scotia, and acted briefly as headmaster of King's Academy until he was inducted as pastor of St. Matthew's Episcopal Church at South Boston in 1838. Sarah's mother Griselda was the daughter of Sarah Apthorp Morton and Richard Cunningham. Sarah Morton was the daughter of Perez Morton, Speaker of the House of Assembly and later Attorney General of Massachusetts, and Sarah Wentworth Apthorp, poetess and great niece of Lady Wentworth. Richard was an influential landowner and merchant from Windsor. Rev. Joseph and Griselda Clinch had six children: John Morton, Sarah Apthorp Cunningham, Mary Josephine (Josey), Mary Griselda (Molly), Edith Clementia, and Joseph Howard (Beppo).

Sarah was raised in South Boston in comfort and privilege. As a refined Victorian lady, she could play the piano and sing, and was often called upon to provide entertainment at social gatherings. But like her mother and father, Sarah received some formal education; beyond the traditional domestic subjects of sewing and reading, she could speak Spanish, German, and French, she could read and write Latin, she studied botany and art, and was an avid reader of novels and poetry.

*William Cranch Bond,
unknown artist, ca. 1840. (see p.4)
Bond (1789-1859) was a Boston
astronomer and clock and watch-
maker. In 1839 he was appointed the
first astronomical observer at Harvard
University and, in 1847, its first director.
Bond and his son George worked closely together,
making the first recognizable daguerreotype of the
Moon and later of the star Vega.*

Like many upper middle-class ladies, Sarah spent much of her time visiting, socializing, and shopping. It was not at all uncommon for ladies of Sarah's class to walk all over Boston and nearby Cambridge to do their shopping or to visit friends. At this time the only form of urban public transportation was the omnibus, a horse-driven shuttle that ran every two hours between Boston and Cambridge. Sarah also attended the theater, musical performances, parties, and balls. She visited the Boston Athenaeum, a private lending library built in 1847 and still in operation today. As the daughter of a minister, religion was central to Sarah's life. Regular church attendance and charitable living were expected; it was not unusual for Sarah to attend church once or twice a day and she volunteered at a local prison, probably reading the Bible to inmates and encouraging their religious and moral education.

While they retained close ties to friends and relatives living in Nova Scotia, Rev. Joseph Clinch and his family made many friends

ASTRONOMICAL OBSERVATORY, CAMBRIDGE, MASS.

"Harvard College Observatory," ca. 1852.

This engraving shows the Harvard University
Observatory much as Sarah would have known it.
The observatory was founded in 1839 with William
Cranch Bond as its first director.
In 1844, a house for the director and his family was con-
structed next to the observatory. This is where Sarah
stayed when visiting the Bond family.
The observatory remains an active part
of the Harvard University campus.

in the Boston area. They were particularly close with the Bond family of South Boston, renowned watchmakers, astronomers, and inventors. William Cranch Bond built the first chronometer in North America (prior to this, chronometers were imported from England and France) and established the observatory at Harvard University. On occasion Sarah visited the observatory, staying overnight in the Bond family home, which was located next to the observatory. The Bond children, especially Richard and Selina, were good friends with Sarah and her siblings.

Family was a focal point for Sarah. Not long before she left for Halifax, Sarah's youngest brother was born. Sarah hated having to leave her baby brother, nick-named Beppo, and she worried about him constantly during her time away. Her siblings and parents were always a foremost concern and the majority of her daily journal entries include mention of mail from them. Sarah became an excellent observer of the merchant and mail vessel signal flags that communicated the arrival of vessels and signalled the possibility of news from home.

Sarah departed Boston on November 15, 1853, accompanied by her cousin Elizabeth (Bella) Bullock, who had been visiting the Clinch family in Boston. It was Bella's family that Sarah lived with during her stay in Halifax. The two young women packed their trunks and booked passage on a steamer for a voyage that lasted three stormy days, much to Sarah's disappointment.

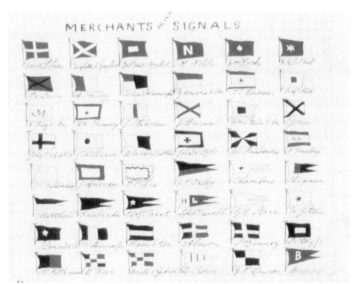

Signal flags were vitally important to nineteenth-century communication in and around Halifax. Flags such as these were flown above the Citadel, informing residents, merchants, and the navy which vessels were entering and departing the harbour.

Boston

"A mingled yarn."

Oct. 1   ✑   I do not expect to have much to put in this, my first attempt at a journal until I reach Halifax and indeed I should not have begun it, unless I had expected to spend the coming winter there. I anticipate so much pleasure and my time is at present wholly taken up with the baby and preparing for my visit. Little Beppo is to be christened tomorrow and I am to receive, for the first time, the Holy Communion from father. It is just a year since Morton and I were confirmed. The first Sunday in October 1852. Mr. & Mrs. Moody, Carry and Lily have come to the christening and will stay until Monday morning.

Oct. 3   ✑   The baby looked sweetly yesterday. He was christened by Bishop Eastburn, who was also his god-father by his proxy. Father Morton was his other god-father and Mrs. Ward his god-mother. He was surrounded with flowers and laughed when the Bishop took him. I was disappointed in the morning that Morton could not kneel on one side of mother as I did on the other, to receive the Holy Communion, but Mr. Moody got between us. Mrs. Moody was too sick to go to church and was in bed the greater part of the day. A good many people came up to see the baby after church & Richard & Selina Bond among the rest. Today I went on to take my lesson. Mr. Johnson found at Reed's the fugues by Bach that I wanted. It was the [indecipherable]. It was a dollar. I went to the school, saw Mr. Wilde, Signor Monti, Madame Doudiet & Father U. Molignon was gone, and I wanted to see him. Mr. Wildes is very sorry I am going to be away this winter, he wanted me to assist him in the school. I dined and spent the rest of the day at the Parks'. Mother came in for a minute with Morton and Beppo on their way from the Bishop's. Mr. Pickman was there in the evening. Dr. Parks is going to New York tomorrow, Mrs. Moody too went home today.

Oct. 4   ✑   I took Beppo down to see Geo. Chadwick this morning, but did not stay very long. The day has been wholly taken up in preparation for Morton's departure tomorrow morning. I think Beppo will miss him almost as much as the rest of us. Only

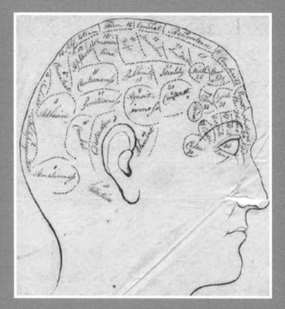

Phrenology Sketch,
attributed to
Dr. Henry Greggs Farish, ca. 1820.

Phrenology is the study of the contours of the
skull as a means of interpreting the character
and mental abilities of a person.
This so-called science was popular
in the mid-nineteenth century.

think! He will be nearly a year old before he sees him again. This has seemed like a very short vacation; it has been so cut up by Mother's visit to Yarmouth N.S. and our consequent dispersion. I drew my third breadth today. I have not had time to do more. Molly is delivering an oration upon Morton's approaching departure. We are expecting James and Mary every day.[1] We were in hopes they would come while Morton was with us.

Oct. 5　　James and Mary not come yet! I have not felt very well today, just sick enough to be very cross and got into a tremendous passion with Molly. Mary Pope has spent the day with us and went to a teachers' meeting this evening with father.

Oct. 6　　Nothing but sewing. Mr. Pons came in this evening, and says Beppo has a very finely balanced head. He says that he has remarked, relating to language, that the organ of tune had as much as that of language to do with it, which was one reason I learned languages so much more easily than the "bumps" give me credit for. Beppo is six months old today.

Oct. 7　　Bella and Beppo took a long walk today. I learned three fugues and tried some voluntaries. Went with Bella to Boston about half past two and staid two hours. We went to Charlotte Bond's, but unfortunately she was out. We went to the Parkses, as I wanted to ask Addie and Cassie to make me some stomachers and to take them some music and embroidery, which Addie wanted for transferring. Mr. Pons called again but did not stay to tea. Mrs. Howe and Minnie called. I went to Mr. Pope's to tea, but soon received an urge to come home for James and Mary have at last arrived. They had to return to the Bromfield House for the night but will come out to stay tomorrow morning. Mother was in bed with a bad severe headache.

Oct. 8　　James and Mary did not come over until nearly one o'clock and I was walking with Mary Pope. When I returned Norman Bond was here with them. Mary is a perfect darling. I love her dearly.

Oct. 9　　Father, Cousin James, and Mary went to Brookline as father officiated for Mr. Stone who has been struck with paralysis. Mr. Wildes preached here. I, fortunately, was at the House of Correction as usual. Mr. Burrill's text was Hebrews VI v.19 "Which hope we have as an anchor of the soul, both sure and steadfast." Mary brought home some beautiful flowers and grapes from Mr. Aspinwall's, where they dinned.

Oct. 10 🐚 I took a music lesson this morning and coming home saw Wendel Phillips at the tea store.[2] Mr. Crane was in the omnibus and told me of Mr. Booth's death. He died on Saturday. In the afternoon, Cousin James, Mary, Bella and I called upon Mrs. Ward. When we came out, it was raining but we were not far from the stand and before we reached home it had stopped. Josey had a whitlow on her thumb which makes her feel very sick.[3] She was very faint several times today.

Oct. 11 🐚 What Josey calls "a real handsome negro" came today with boots and slippers. Josey and I each took a pair of boots. I was going to see Addie Parks this afternoon, but they came here before I started out, and staid to tea. They brought me three stomachers they made for me, they had to go home at eight o'clock. Bella and I went to Mr. Grantham's to ask about the *Bloomer*. The trip after next will probably be the first of November and we will go then.

Oct. 12 🐚 Cousin James and Mary went to Dr. Hitchcock this morning and must go again tomorrow. They went to Cambridge with father and Bella. Mr. Bond was over Monday and appointed today to go. Molly and I walked around S. Boston on errands this afternoon to try and cure my head-ache but did not succeed.

Oct. 13 🐚 Cousin James and Mary had a delightful evening at Cambridge last night. They saw the moon, Jupiter, and all the different beauties in Lysa (viz. Alpha Lysa, the double or rather quadruple star and the nebula). They have been again to Dr. H's today and have gone this evening to the Museum, accompanied by Bella, Josey, Molly and Hubert Pope. I threw the baby's coral hitch-ups into the fire this evening, mistaking them for apple parings in the low light. It was stupid enough to be sure, but that is nothing uncommon. I worked the lowest row of one breadth this eve.

Oct. 14 🐚 I went into town with Bella to shop this morning, but did not succeed very well as I did not take any money with me, trusting to ask father for some and he had none either, so he had to borrow $10 from Mr. Wildes. I went then with father, bought a comb, (I broke mine this morn.) some linen cambric for Lily, a raw silk for myself, and one like it for a birthday present to Bella from us all, some shibet for a talma and a pair of hitch-ups for Beppo. I was very fortunate in matching them for Ford had but one pair of clasps like those I burned. When I came home I found Cousin James had brought me a beautiful winter bonnet, dark blue, the most becoming one I ever wore. Bella says our silk is just the plaid worn by the 72nd who are now in Halifax. Quite a coincidence. Mrs. Wallace called this evening upon Mary bringing her a beautiful glass basket.

Oct. 15 ⊰ I am so tired! I have been all day with Mary, Mrs. Caines & Wallace in the Athenaeum. We have had a pleasant but fatiguing day. James & Mary expected to go today but fortunately the wind was ahead and will stay until Monday.

Oct. 16 ⊰ I did not see Cousin James before I went to church this morning, but left a message with Mary for them to come down to see House of Correction, and watched for them in vain all church time, and when I returned home, I found they went this morning. It was so provoking for they will have to stay in the harbour until tomorrow morning, just as mother did.

Oct. 22 ⊰ Nothing but sewing and going down to the church to practice with Josey (as she is to play next Sunday) until last night "cressâ dies nota," when I went to Gottschalk's concert. Unfortunately just while we were impatient by awaiting Gottschalk's appearance, according to the programme, Herr Helmsmüller came forward, bowing and scraping and 'announced with much regret' that Mr. Gottschalk had that moment received a 'note announcing the death of his father. He would not however disappoint us.' He (Mr. Helmsmüller) left it to us to imagine how well a person could play under the "circumstances." Circumstances included, I would have listened to him, as long as he would have been willing to play to me without the least approach to weariness, in spite of the wise, technical, false criticism of the "Transcript." It only shows that no degree of sentiment can be appreciated or felt by some people. These soi-disant excellence, no depth of lovers or rather connoisseurs of the "divine art," think that they show their learning, and make the multitude stare by a liberal use of techni-

Louis Moreau Gottschalk, ca. 1860

Louis Moreau Gottschalk was a French-speaking American pianist and song-
writer. The first American musician to become internationally famous as a
composer and pianist, Gottschalk was only twenty-four years old when he gave
his Boston performance, which was particularly important in his career. Just
before the performance, an announcement was made that his father had died.
Until this time, Gottschalk's family had been supported by his father. The
young artist began touring extensively throughout Europe, North American,
and South America to support his family. While touring Brazil he contracted
yellow fever and on December 18, 1869 at age forty, he died at the piano
while rehearsing his work Morte.[4]

Boston

cal terms that they don't half understand. The idea of anyone listening to the improvisation (I think) that Gottschalk played when he was encored and saying that he "lacked repose and breadth of style" was perfectly absurd. And even Aptommas "The celebrated Welsh Harpist" whom they condescended to admire, they dammed with faint praise. I can not conceive how the harp could be better played, or the music better appreciated and feelingly, understandingly rendered. Bocha was a mere beginner compared to him and he is very young indeed. I could hardly breathe until he finished. I did not like Mlle Brehrend at all. I could have sung as well myself. She has power, but no sweetness, no melody, no expression, no grace. I did not like the last piece that Gottschalk played, a grand fantasia on Lucia di Lammermoor by Light.[5] It was nothing but darting from one end of the piano to the other; a show off piece I suppose. I have begun to embroider my talma today and am delighted with it. I only did a few stitches.

Oct. 23   Father exchanged with Mr. Burrill today as I wanted to hear him once before I go to Halifax. He could not dine there, much to my disappointment, as he was sent for to attend a funeral between churches. He performed the burial service down there for a convict who died yesterday. So he has had a hard days work. Capt Robbins spoke of my going to Halifax, and is willing to have Josey as my substitute while I am away. He is very kind indeed and so is Mr. Burrill and I like them both very much.

Oct. 25   A day to be remembered in my list of bright spots, or rather of brilliant ones on what has my whole life been but one bright tissue. But what renders today particularly bright is that I was able to go to Jullien's concert.[6] I thought that if I went to Gottschalk's, I could not go to the other, and had therefore given up even all hopes of it, but Mr. Pope bought a family ticket & having a spare one, gave it to me. Our party consisted of Mrs. Pope, Mrs. Blackmore, Alexander, Mary, Bella & me. I was delighted. Mr. Collinit, the leader of Napoleon 1st's Court Balls in 1812, performed on the flageolet. We were particularly fortunate in hearing him as he is very celebrated, very old, and will retire from public life, after this one engagement. I was so pleased, as well as surprised with Jullien. He is very like his portraits to be sure, but he has a remarkably gentlemanly air in which his likenesses are certainly "found wanting." His power over his orchestra make his Baton appear like a magic wand, so wonderful are the results. Positively, you can almost see the melody gushing from the point of it and can hardly persuade yourself that the instruments are providing the sounds instead of the wand. I never saw an audience so completely carried away. But yet with all that, the music was not of such high order as Gottschalk's & great as is my pleasure at being able to go to both, yet when I thought I could have but one, I felt I made a wise choice in preferring Gottschalk.

Nov. 12　Finished my talma, and I think I say a good deal is saying that is nearly equaled my anticipations. Though, truth to tell, it would not have done so, but for the kindness of Mrs. Moody, who put it onto the lining after I had finished the embroidery. I was a fortnight working it and shall wear it today to Mr. Bond's where I am going to say good-bye for we are going next Monday. I shall stay all night at the Observatory & come home tomorrow morning, call to bid good-bye to Mrs. Ward, the Williamses, & Parkses & Dr. Hitchcock and get Charlotte's fans. &c &c.

Nov. 14　The 25th Sunday after Trinity. My last at home. If I could but be at home. But alas! My last Sunday must be spent among convicts & law-breakers, so I thought this morning, little thinking how fully my thoughts were to be carried out. The most violent storm of the season has been today and I can not but feel very thankful to find myself safe at home, instead of being tossed about upon "the world of waters", as we should have been if the *Halifax* as was its original intention, had started yesterday. I have been five months at the House of Correction, and it is the first time it has stormed & it stormed to some purpose, for we were obliged to stay to tea as Capt. Robbins would not even send us in a carriage in such a storm. Mr. Irwin, one of the officers of the prison, solicited the honor & pleasure &c. &c. of driving us home, which soon we most graciously (making a virtue of as not unpleasant necessity) vouchsafe to grant.

Nov. 15　Went to bid Madam Eastham good-bye, while Mother & Mary packed my trunk. When I was leaving her, she gave me a set of garnet & pearls, a ring, broach & earrings, very pretty, a beautiful lace cape & a pair of undersleeves. Very useful & desirable additions to my stock of pretty things. I met a Miss Dora Clark there, I believe the daughter of B.C. Clark. We go at six o'clock this evening.

Halifax
at
Mid-century

Mid nineteenth-century Halifax was a city of change and growth. As a strategic port for the British forces, war-time Halifax was a bustling place. The constant military presence provided entrepreneurial Haligonians with numerous business opportunities. Soldiers and sailors needed places to eat, shop, and of course socialize. Early in the history of Nova Scotia, bars, brothels, and other less-respectable businesses emerged. Other industries such as timber and shipbuilding provided fortunes for upper-class investors and seasonal employment for working-class labourers. A new middle class had begun to evolve in Nova Scotia, and the landed gentry, who had been granted large tracts of land in the eighteenth century, found their social circles changing. Mercantile families were prospering and began to take leading roles in church and state.

Religion and politics had always been deeply intertwined in Nova Scotia's history. As the established church since the founding of Halifax in 1749, the Church of England had been the official church of the military and the government. However, in 1848 the bishop of Nova Scotia was no longer provided a seat in govern-

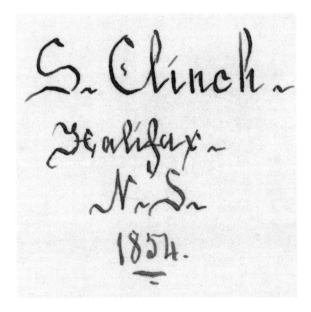

ment and in 1854 the Government of Nova Scotia ceased contributions to Episcopal funds. It was then that the government declared its independence from the church. Despite the official removal of the church from matters of state, years of close ties meant that religion still played an important role in the social and political life of Halifax and Nova Scotia.

Since its founding, the city of Halifax—a strategic Atlantic port—had been a transitory home to thousands of British sailors and soldiers. Beginning in the late 1820s, a large contingent of military engineers was stationed in Halifax to give the run-down Citadel a much needed facelift. The presence of these officers and men from various companies contributed to Halifax's character; the spin-off of this presence, however, was not always positive. Barrack Street (now Brunswick Street) was a notorious part of town, supporting grog shops and brothels. Drunken brawls among sailors and soldiers on city streets were not unheard of.

In 1853 the outbreak of the war in the Crimean between Russia and a coalition of Great Britain, France, Sardinia, and Turkey meant that Halifax was again a point of departure for soldiers heading into battle. Numerous soldiers and officers (some of them known to Sarah) were posted to Turkey. The initial excitement felt by the forces in Halifax quickly turned to worry as news of injuries and fatalities reached those left behind.

Throughout the first half of the century a stream of immigration also left its mark on the city. Racism and discrimination often made it difficult for immigrants to find employment in a city so closely aligned to the British crown. Many of the city's residents faced poverty, and deadly diseases such as cholera and smallpox occasionally swept through the city. Life, even for the upper classes, was not always one of complete luxury. The city's streets were not paved and were often muddy and barely passable, or, in winter, icy and snow covered. Pedestrian and carriage travel could be treacherous. Those who could afford it warmed their homes with coal and lit them with gas. These relatively new industries were not without their troubles. Residents who relied on coal were at the mercy of mine productivity and vessels that transported the coal. Gas, which often replaced oil, could have an unpleasant odour when lit, especially in rooms with little or no air circulation.

Despite some physical blemishes, mid-century Halifax had begun to take on the appearance of an urban community. An elegant sandstone building, Province House, had been built in 1819 to accommodate the province's legislative assembly, giving the provincial capital a more impressive appearance. Halifax was home to the province's governor, who also resided in a grand sandstone home. The city was incorporated in 1841 and Stephen Binney served as its first mayor, followed in 1843 by beer baron Alexander Keith. The Public Gardens had been established by the Horticultural Society, and Point Pleasant Park, though still home to some British regiments, provided a place for socializing and sleighrides. Downs' zoological garden at the base of the North West Arm offered residents a chance to view such exotic animals as peacocks and bears.

Communication by mail was dependent on sail and steam vessels, but by mid-century the telegraph was providing Haligonians with a faster and more reliable method of communication. For local, national, and international news, the residents of Halifax had several newspapers to choose from; the *Acadian Recorder* and the *Halifax Chronicle* were two of the largest local papers, and the *Presbyterian Witness* was one of the many religious journals available to the reading public.

Reverend William Bullock, ca. 1865. Bullock was responsible for the establishment of four churches in Digby, and he became the first rector of St. Luke's Church in Halifax.

Two colleges had been established in Halifax and numerous public, private, and church-run schools were open to the city's more fortunate children. In 1831 the Mechanics' Institute was established as a post-graduate vehicle for intellectual discussions on a variety of topics, excluding politics and religion. Drawn from Halifax's middle and upper classes, members gathered for discussion and to hear presentations. Women were permitted to attend meetings but not to present papers. The institute evolved into what is now known as the Nova Scotia Museum. Clearly, by mid-century, Halifax had become more than a colonial outpost significant only in times of war.

This was the Halifax that greeted Sarah when she arrived in November 1853. Reverend William Bullock met his daughter Bella and niece Sarah on the wharf upon their arrival after a three-day voyage from Boston. William Bullock was the husband of Sarah's paternal aunt, Mary Clinch. Prior to his appointment as curate of St. Paul's Church in Halifax, Bullock lived an extraordinary life. Born in Prittwell, England, he joined the Royal Navy where he eventually earned the rank of lieutenant. He witnessed several battles during his time in the navy, but was influenced more by his station in Newfoundland, where he was assigned to a hydrographic survey. During this time he was greatly moved by the missionary work being undertaken by the Society for the Propagation of the Gospel. He also had the opportunity to befriend his future father-in-law, Revered Dr. John Clinch, a British medical doctor accredited with administering the first smallpox inoculation in Canada. Clinch was close friends with Edward Jenner, the doctor who developed the smallpox vaccine, and sent him some of the vaccine to use in his mission at Trinity. Clinch first inoculated his own children prior to providing the service to the community.

Mrs. Mary Bullock, ca. 1870

Bullock was discharged from the navy for health reasons and returned to England to study religion. In 1822 he was ordained deacon and quickly advanced to the priesthood. Returning to Newfoundland, he was appointed by the bishop of Nova Scotia to the mission of Twillingate, and later, to Trinity Bay. Popular with the people of his extensive coastal mission, Bullock attended to them by piloting a small boat. He also offered medical services, including surgery, which were self-taught using the medical books and instruments willed to him by the late Dr. Clinch, who died in 1819. Less than a year after coming to Newfoundland, William Bullock married Mary Clinch. Bullock was appointed coroner at Trinity Bay before his religious appointment to Digby Parish in 1841. Bishop John Inglis appointed Bullock curate of St. Paul's Cathedral in 1847 to replace Rev. William Cogswell. Bullock was happy to remove to Halifax, as he was eager for his children to benefit from the educational opportunities the growing city had to offer.

The Bullock family lived in a modest home at 66 South Street on a property that boasted a kitchen garden, a backyard, and a small stable. William and Mary had ten children, several of whom

Corner of South and Queen streets, ca. 1870.
The Bullock home was located at 66 South Street, near the corner of
South and Queen streets, across from Fort Massey Cemetery (foreground).
McQueen Manor presently stands in its former location.

Sarah mentions repeatedly in her journals: William Henry, Charles Beverly, Mary Brenton, Charlotte Frances, Louisa, Josey, and Reginald Heber. Several of her cousins were adolescents at the time of her visit, and would have been a constant presence in the Bullock home. Also living for a time in the house was Heber's former classmate and friend Todd Jones. Jones was a constant visitor to the Bullock home before he became quite ill and took up residence with the family permanently.

As the daughter of an Episcopalian minister, Sarah adjusted easily to the religious and social commitments that accompanied life in the Bullock home. Bullock not only had duties at St. Paul's Church, but he also preached at St. Luke's Chapel of Ease, and several times a month across the North West Arm to the congregation at Falkland (now Purcells Cove). He also served as military chaplain at the prison on Melville Island and at the poor house. In these duties he was greatly assisted by his son Heber, who was also a curate at St. Paul's.

Heber graduated from King's College, where his father was a member of the Board of Directors, and was ordained to the deaconate in 1852 by Bishop Hibbert Binney. He also served for a

Reverend Heber Bullock, ca. 1870

time as private secretary to the Lieutenant Governor Lord Mulgrave. In 1855 he was appointed chaplain to the sailors and soldiers stationed at Halifax.

The prominent role of the Church of England directly influenced the social position of the Bullock family in Nova Scotia, requiring them to meet a never-ending list of social obligations such as invitations to visit friends, relatives, and congregants and to attend parties and balls. Bullock was an energetic man, hardworking and respected by all who knew him. He was a poet, a man of strong values, and beloved by his family, as evinced by Sarah's repeated praise for him.

While in Halifax Sarah made many friends and spent much of her time socializing. Typical days during her visit included a shopping trip downtown or a walk to Point Pleasant Park, attending a church service at St. Paul's Church or St. Luke's to hear her uncle or cousin speak, and visiting with friends and congregants. Bullock was vice-president of the St. Paul's Visiting Society, which no doubt contributed to the Bullock family's full social calendar. Bullock occasionally preached at the Garrison Chapel, the official church for officers and soldiers stationed at Halifax. (His position may have allowed his entrance by permit into the Citadel, which was normally closed to most city residents.)

Sarah's calling list contained the names of some of the most influential families in mid-century Halifax. The children of Judge William Blowers and Sarah Bliss were constant companions for Sarah and her cousins. Judge Bliss was a member of the legislative assembly, a puisine judge of the Supreme Court, a governor of King's College, and a trustee of the Halifax Grammar School; he sat on the first board of directors for the Bank of Nova Scotia, and was a faithful member of St. Paul's and later St. Luke's parishes. The Bliss family maintained homes in both Halifax and Windsor, and Sarah was a regular guest at both. Sarah's social circle also included the Allison and Almon families. Charles (Charlie) Almon was the son of Mather and Sophia Pryor Almon. Mather was a graduate of King's College, a prominent Halifax merchant, banker, governor of Dalhousie University and King's College, and a member of the legislative assembly. Charlie was the cousin of another constant in Sarah's life, Willie de Blois, who became a successful Halifax lawyer. The Almons were also devoted members of St. Paul's Church.

Throughout her visit to the Annapolis Valley, Sarah spent time with members of Thomas Chandler Haliburton's family. Haliburton and his first wife Louisa, who died in 1841, had ten children, many of whom Sarah was acquainted with.[1] Many of the Haliburton children divided their time between Windsor and Halifax. During Sarah's stay, T.C. Haliburton still resided at Clifton, his Windsor home; however, he removed to England in 1856 with his second wife. Sarah also kept company with the Halliburton family (note spelling), especially Chief Justice Brenton Halliburton, his wife Margaret (the daughter of Bishop Charles Inglis), and their nine children. Members of the Uniacke family, known to many Nova Scotians, were also companions to Sarah and members of her family. The Uniacke family had ties to the Anglican Church, as Rev. Robert Fitz-Uniacke was the rector of St. George's Church.

Louisa and Charlotte Bullock, ca. 1870

Sarah's days often included a visit from her seamstress, Mrs. Morrisey, who came to the Bullock home regularly to help Sarah and her female cousins make dresses and accessories. Clothing and accessories like gloves and hankerchiefs were central to a young Victorian woman's life. Sarah spent rainy afternoons or occasional evenings by the fire working on sewing projects such as the embroidery of a "stomacher"—the bodice of a dress that attaches to the skirt. Many diary entries mention dress materials such as tartlan or silk. Sarah had enough skill to perform small repairs to her clothing, to alter bonnets, and to make small cloaks called mantles. However, to construct a complete gown, she required the assistance of a professional like Mrs. Morrisey.

Dinner parties—with dancing and music lasting late into the evening following dinner—were popular among Victorians. During the holiday season much of Halifax's social elite attended fancy balls, typically one at Province House and one hosted by the Royal Engineers, and spent New Year's Day entertaining a steady stream of visitors. Games came into fashion during the Victorian period, and Sarah passed many an evening playing games such as bagatelle, a modified version of billiards. Like most aspects of Victorian life, game playing had well-defined rules of behaviour. The height of ill manners was to show anger or frustration, even if the opponent was found cheating. The good Victorian guest took part in charades as assigned by the hostess, even if the charade was obscure or distasteful. As Sarah noted, the practice of group behaviour was not always easy: "We went to Mrs. Lyttleton's last night…did not enjoy it much particularly as M. Tuck Grigor, whom I do not like at all, trapped me into a game of chess, a most stupid thing to do at a party" (April 25, 1854).

Sarah also concentrated on personal betterment. She studied Latin, math, and other academic subjects with her cousin Heber. She also helped her younger cousins with reading, writing, and math. As a well-rounded young lady, Sarah could play the piano and sing, but she also enjoyed art. She was enrolled in drawing classes given by a local artist, Mary McKie. Sarah studied art with a good friend of the Bullock family, Dr. William Grigor. She was curious about the city and took any opportunity she could find to travel to new parts, to attend military events, or to meet new people.

Nov. 18. Halifax!

Nov. 18   Halifax! Three such days as I have passed, may it be long before I see again! I never suffered so much from sea-sickness before. When I went to Yarmouth it lasted but a few hours. But this time I could not leave my berth without assistance & not stand upon the deck at all until this morning and then only with the captain's assistance (whom I nearly dragged down once) inspired by the sight of Halifax Harbor & city. We saw Uncle William on the wharf. When we reached home they were not expecting us, Uncle William having gone down only on the chance of our being there. The house at first looked deserted but at last we heard Louisa singing, and guided by that we very soon found a welcome, warm as heart could wish. Weak & tired as I was, I could hardly help having a hearty cry. It would have seemed such a relief. But dear Charlotte, ever mindful of others, soon had the bath in readiness for us & everything we wanted, & then when refreshed by it, she had some tea & toast (not Mrs. Bamble's[2]) ready for us, for well she knew that all we eat on board would not destroy our appetite at all, such as it was so with me, for I was too sick to attempt to taste any thing but some tea until the third & last day when I took half a cup of soup.

View of Halifax from Bullock Home, ca. 1870.

Nov. 19   Still very dizzy from the effects of the sea-sickness. It really is not safe for me to go up the stairs alone. I almost fell frequently! Mr. Jones came up today and staid three hours. He is much better, but it is the first time he has been able to come up since his illness. I went down town for walk, but was too sick & dizzy to enjoy it much. I was agreeably surprised in Mr. Jones. He seems to take pleasure & interest in giving information, where an opportunity occurs, not only to the older ones, but to draw the attention of Bella and me also, for anything of interest or information, and takes pains to explain anything, as clearly as possible.

Nov. 20   Sunday next before Advent. Sacrament Sunday. I was very glad to have my first Sunday in Halifax, Sacrament Sunday. Heber led and Uncle William preached both morning and afternoon. I like Uncle William's preaching very much indeed. I love him dearly, as how can I help doing, and all the family too. They are taken as a whole, the most amiable & united family I ever met with. Cousin Ben called at noon to see me, and went to church with us. I am disappointed in him. He is handsome but very conceited and coy combined. Perhaps I shall like him better on further acquaintance. He has got most bravely over the bashfulness that fairly overwhelmed him when he was with us, two or three years ago. Willie de Blois, for the first time since Josey's departure, sat in view of our pew. In the afternoon, he came again, bringing Charlie Almon with him Mr. Parsons was startled just as if he had seen a ghost, when he saw me sitting in Josey's old seat in church, & as it rained, I wore my green bonnet with which I have to have my hair down, which increased considerably the likeness (which is thought here very strong), between me and Josey. Returning from church in the afternoon we met Mrs. General Gore to whom I was introduced.[3] She talks very much like Georgina Haliburton so much, that she almost looks like her. I have written to Uncle Morton and Aunt Eliza this eve. The letters will go tomorrow morning and they will probably receive them at night.

William DeBlois, ca. 1865. William was from a prominent Halifax family and married Jane Pryor.

Nov. 21 ❧ I went shopping today, and spent twenty-two shillings. I bought a portmanteau (having ruined mine on board). I shall keep the old one to keep coppers in. I got a bottle of [indecipherable] to send to father, as I was making a parcel to send home by Capt. O'Brien. I went down again this afternoon to see him and give him my letters & I was very glad to see him again for I felt very grateful to him for all his kindness to me while coming. He has also taken charge of Mrs. Ward's dressing case. "Mischief" as Bella calls the mate, found a velvet rosette she had lost, and returned it to her.

Nov. 22 ❧ Rained all day. I am hardly yet settled enough to sit down and sew and am still too dizzy and my head aches too much to do much of anything. I have been reading Tougue's "Magi King." It is a mere story not to be compared to "Nadine." I was disappointed. I was well laughed at to day when looking to see how much sewing I had done. I found out that I had cut out six eyelits ready for working! How industrious I am growing! Heber brought me home a bottle of [indecipherable], because I had sent mine to father, and a little tiny corkscrew to open it with.

Nov. 23 ❧ Wednesday. We went to the Citadel today. Uncle William got a permit and the party consisting of Uncle William, Mr. Halliburton, Bella, Miriam, Fred, Willie, Charlotte and me, started about half past twelve. We returned about half past two very tired and very merry. We were weighed there and to my better astonishment I weigh one hundred and thirty two! Only one pound less than Bella. We went under ground more than a mile and a half. I never saw any fortifications before. We came back through Artillery Park and the artillery were just going down to the chain battery for ball practice.[4] When we returned home we found several callers. The Wainwrights, the Misses Chipman &c. Mrs. Judge Hill came in and I never in my life saw such a resemblance between any two persons, between her and [indecipherable]. I was delighted with her. Afterwards we went shopping accepting some commissions for Mr. Halliburton. We did not succeed very well being hurried home by a shower. Met the much talked of Charlie Almon on horseback. Miriam stopped to ask him about his sister who had been sick and he was introduced to me. He says he is coming up soon, our visiting list amounts now to seventeen.

*"Officers of the 76th Regiment
in Front of Officers' Mess at Citadel," 1871*

Nov. 24   At home, Thanksgiving day! I quite forgot it until dinner which reminded me of it. Charlie Almon came up this evening. I like him pretty well. He appears quite unaffected and not at all foppish. We ate chestnuts and apples and torment-ed the poor boy by talking of Josey's admirers at home. I sang a lit-tle, but was sadly out of voice. The steamer came in today.

Nov. 25   I have received letters, the first since I came. One from father with a postscript from mother, and one from Aunt Eliza.[5] Cousin Ben brought the last, merely a note. Father's letter brought the sad news that Beppo is suffering very much from teething has had to have his gums lanced. Poor little thing! It does seem dreadful for such delicate little creatures to suffer so and they can't understand it and don't know how to bear it. Though Beppo certainly bears pain better than any baby I ever saw. The Darling! I hope he will soon be better. Teeth are a continual trouble and tor-ture from the time they begin to come, till we have entirely lost them. Bella has had the dressmaker today, Miss Morrisey, and if she succeeds with me as well as she has with her, I shall be more than satisfied. I have written to Mother, Lina Bond& Addie Parks, to go by Mr. Halliburton tomorrow, also to Aunt Eliza.

Nov. 26   Bella and I walked round the Point with Heber. I came back very tired, but better for it. I borrowed an extra

The artist, James Bland, sketched several scenes of his life in Halifax and was a friend of Sarah's. This is much how Point Pleasant Park would have looked during Sarah's stay, as it was still in constant use by the military for training and as a residence.

"Encampment of Artillery and 76th Regiment at Point Pleasant," Lieut.-Colonel James Fox Bland, 1855

pair of gloves Heber happened to have in his pocket for my hands were cold, so tonight I found a pair of plush gloves, from him, with a Latin inscription. So I went to his door and called out a Latin answer through the keyhole. I have worn them before and they are the warmest things imaginable. I think I shall send a pair to Josey for Christmas. I hope Beppo is better.

Nov. 27   First Sunday in Advent. Uncle William had a dreadful headache this morning, but would go to church but only read the Ante Communion service. This afternoon he did not go at all. Heber read and Mr. Maturin preached. I can't bear him. He pronounces strangely and his voice is so very peculiar that I can't understand one word in ten that he says. Aunt Mary said it was an excellent sermon. Went to St. Paul's this evening. Mr. Maturin read and the Archdeacon preached. I was introduced to the Archdeacon after church. Charlie Almon and Jim Twining walked home with us. Jim Twining is a dreadful fop.[6] I like Charlie Almon very much.

Nov. 28   Been shopping and calling all day. I bought a pair of gloves for Josey, a coque de perle brooch for Molly; two pair of socks for Beppo, three handkerchiefs for Father, and a necktie for Morton. Some black Coburg for a jacket for myself and priced some Australian crêpes, as I want to send a dress of it to

mother, as there is no such material in Boston. This afternoon I called with Bella upon Emma Carman and Miss Grove. We found Uncle William there and met Dr. Grigor Sr. coming out. Met Robert Duport in the street and did not recognize him.

Nov. 29   Tuesday. Bought mother's dress, was very tired when I came back but met Heber on the way home & went in and saw his

Reverend Edward Maturin, ca.1875. Rev. Edward Maturin was curate of St. Paul's Parish. He, William Bullock, and Heber Bullock often shared the preaching duties at St. Paul's.

school. Mr. Jones was here when we came home. He staid to lunch. Walked down to the round tower with Heber and came home through the woods. The Misses Grove and Miss Boggs came to tea and Charlie Almon and Jim Twining came in after tea. I like Charlie Almon very much indeed he is so unaffected and quiet. Jim Twining is a dreadful fop.

Nov. 30 St. Andrews Day. This evening the military have their ball. I could have gone if I wished, but Aunt Mary and the others having declined, I thought I should rather not go without them, and if possible, I should like my "coming out" to be either at Government House or some more private ball. Miriam went down town to look for a crochet case for a Christmas present to Mary Pope, but could not get one under three dollars and a half. Just what I gave for mother's dress. So I had to give up all thoughts of it. It snowed a little today.

Dec. 1 Henceforth, my little journal, you must be locked up as what I have now to write in you is not to be seen by others. I had been out walking with Miriam, and found a letter awaiting one I would not imagine whose writing it was and never looking to see where it was dated, began it aloud, but before I read two lines I stopped short, hoping most devoutly that it might be some trick of Morton and Josey but the remainder and signature convinced me too well of its sincerity. Nothing that could have happened to me could have given me more pain and sorrow causing, as I can hardly hope it will not, a breach between us, and such pleasant friends. I had rather it had been anyone else. It was all the more embarrassing from my being away from home, and out of reach of mother's counsel and it was so completely unexpected and undreamed of, that I could have neither prevented it, or ask her about it before I came. The only thing I could do and which I did, was to [send] her a copy, asking her to answer it in the negative. It has made one feel so unsettled and unhappy. Probably more than it otherwise would, but that I was not very well and had been suffering from a severe headache caused, I think, by cold, for several days previous. He is so quiet and we had known each other so long (from early childhood) and I am so young, yes a school girl, that such an idea never entered my head. I am so sorry. It seems as if I had only had the least intimation of it, I might have prevented it last summer when I was there. I was so happy in being able to number them among my best and dearest friends, that it seems

"Dr. Wm Grigor,"
William Valentine, 1838

A prestigious Halifax surgeon, Dr. William Grigor Sr.
became Halifax County Coroner and personal doctor to
Joseph Howe. He founded the first Halifax dispensary to
aid the poor, which today provides outpatient services at
the IWK Grace Hospital. Both Grigor and his wife,
Catherine Louise Forman, took an interest in art, and
Grigor was an amateur artist, occasionally taking lessons
with Sarah.

very hard to break with them so I should as soon have expected Heber, or Mr. Bond to write me such a letter and yet cannot name a fault in him, except his delicate health. I might wait long before finding one half so good, and if I did, perhaps they would not so overrate me as I fear he has done. Aunt Mary to whom I showed the letter said it was one I might be proud of, but "Love is not in our power. Nay, what seems strange, is not in our choice. We only love where Fate ordains we should. And blindly fond, oft slight superior merit." I hope and pray that I have not done wrong, or decided too hastily but I do not think I could have done otherwise.[7]

Dec. 2 🖎 I am almost too tired and sick to write. I did not sleep a quarter of an hour all night. I had such a headache. We went to Mrs. Binney's to tea last night which did not make me feel much better, sick as I felt before I went and I thought I should never get home.[8] Today we called on Mrs. Fitz-Uniacke but did not see her, on Rev. George Hill,[9] to carry him a book, and on Mrs. & Lilly Moren & the Misses Newton, very nice people. We called on the Chipmans and Fairbankses but did not find them at home. We stopped in the street to speak to Lilly Allison, and Mr. Hardy stared out of a window opposite until we turned away. Perhaps he was looking to see the resemblance, believed in here, between me and Josey. Finished my Journal letter to Mother this evening and found it to consist of fourteen pages of layer letter paper besides a sheet to father enclosing an Indian dialect version of the Lord's Prayer and a note to Mrs. Ward. Tomorrow, I will make up my bundle as the *Belle* goes on Monday.

Dec. 3 🖎 A violent snow storm. I made up my parcel, and a pretty respectable one it was too. We were to take tea at the Groves' tonight but the storm was too much for us. Miriam and I polished up our writing desks today and they look as good as new. While I am writing, Heber is copying poetry into my scrap book. I received a letter from Mother and Morton yesterday and one from Aunt Eliza today, enclosing one from mother. Uncle Morton has not answered me yet. I wish he would. I shall wait very anxiously for Mother's next letter.

Dec. 4 🖎 Second Sunday in Advent. When we were going to church Heber said that the *Halifax* would probably leave Boston this morning and if so, she will be here Wednesday or

Mrs. Mary Bullock, ca. 1870

Mary was the daughter of Dr. John and Hannah Clinch, and the sister of Sarah's father, Rev. Joseph Clinch. She was raised in Trinity, Newfoundland, where she met and married a friend of her father's, William Bullock.

Thursday, I hope she will bring me a great many letters. Mother cannot have received the letter I sent by mail Friday morning in time to answer it by the *Halifax*. I wish she could, but it takes six days by mail. It was the quickest way I could send it, as the steamer was not in, [and it] is the best in the particular case. I must wait patiently I suppose, until the *Bloomer* or *Belle* returns. I sang in the choir today for the first time, Mr. Parson's turned completely round and stared. He was astonished I suppose not to see me in my (Josey's) old place in the corner. We are busy practicing for Christmas. Tuesday week will be Heber's birthday. I shall get him either "Essays of Elia," or "Southeys Curse of Kuharna," he was so delighted with the quaint motto of the last when I told it to him yesterday. It is a very true one and beautifully illustrated by the poem "Curses are like chickens, they always come home to roost." I was too tired to go to St. Paul's tonight, so I staid at home to write. Heber, Uncle William, Bella and Tory went.

Dec. 5   Rose at sunrise, for a wonder, Heber calling me and felt more comfortable all day after it. Mr. Jones came over today, and staid to lunch. Heber and I walked down to the round tower, and when I came back, Aunt and Charlotte went with me to call upon Lady Le Marchant.[10] She was just going out sleighing, so we did not see her but had my name written upon her books and that was all I wanted. We saw her and Sir Gaspard in the street.

Dec. 6   Walked with Heber. Several callers among others, Mrs. Charles Murdock, who came to ask Tory, Bella, Heber, and me to tea tonight. We went and had a very pleasant evening. She had one book called "Beauties of the Opera and Ballet." Some were really exquisite. The prettiest were Carlotta Grisé, and La Gisella Guiletta Grisé, as Norma and Danny Ceritó as Ondine and Taglioùi as La Sylphide. We came home at about ten o'clock. Beppo is eight months old.

Dec. 7   Wednesday. Mother ought to receive the letter I mailed last Friday this afternoon. I hope she has. I wish I could hear from her. I must wait nearly a week, if not more, for an answer to it. If I could but see her for a few moments and ask her about it, it [would] be so much more satisfactory. It rained last night, and today it is very muddy. I went down town today three times and was muddy enough, and tired too when I came back.

Uncle William has gone to Mr. Collinses to a dinner and Aunt Mary, Charlotte & Louisa have gone to Mrs. Chipmans to tea. Heber has just gone after them. Anna Steven's has been here this evening and we acted charades. The costumes, being totally impromptu would have made a fastidious person stare. My head ached terribly, and I did not much like it, but I am glad enough to have been able to stay at home even, for you have to exert yourself more when you are away from home, or rather at a stranger's, but here there were four to entertain one, so it was not so hard. Tomorrow we are invited to a musical party at Mrs. James Gray's and Friday to dinner at Mrs. Fitz-Uniacke's. Cousin Ben said he was going. It is a dinner party. I saw him today when I was down town with Heber. I went into his office to see it. His den as he calls it. He gave me a parcel from Aunt Eliza, which Rev. Porter brought up from Windsor. I must write to her & thank her for a bow, wristers and a woolen mufflers because Mr. Porter goes back tomorrow. I don't feel much like it, for I am very sleepy indeed. There was a brigantine signaled today. I do hope it is the *Halifax*, but I am afraid it is not possible. I hope mother will answer my letter as quick as she can. I got a bottle of lavender water for mother today, at Langley's.[11] I like Langley very much, he is so civil. I saw the wonderful Vernon Jones yesterday. He escorted us to Mrs. Murdock's and is only a boy about sixteen or eighteen years old.

Dec. 8 & I spent all the morning in arranging my dress to go to Mrs. Gray's and I found it a harder matter than I had anticipated. Miriam has dressed in black silk, low with an illusion skirt, also black, a white, scarlet and gold bow, and black velvet in her hair. She looked very well indeed. Bella wore her blue Austrian hair crepe, and I my raw silk & diamonds. I was introduced to Capt. Gore, Capt. Barry, Will de Blois, Mr. Bland & Mr. Maturin and a Miss McLane, the Boston Belle as she is called by what right I do not know, unless by the rule of contraries. She is a fine, showy looking girl, but with the most forward, unrefined manners I ever saw in polite society. I like Capt. Barry and Mr. Martin very much. Mr. Martin walked home with us. There was a Mr. Ich there who sang very well indeed. Miss McLane played and sang. Her playing is very brilliant but her time and taste are very bad. Her voice is very highly cultivated & she would sing well if she were not so very, very affected and self conceited. She closes her teeth and parts her lips while singing. Every word and every action is for effect. I danced with Mr. Blanch, the first quadrille, Will de Blois the second. Will de Blois, "La Tempete" and Mr. Martin, "Pop goes the Weasel" and "Roger de Coverly." Altogether I enjoyed myself very much. Will de Blois sentiment slipped and prosed dreadfully about Josey & Halifax and Josey's admirers here and I paid him back in his own coin, by telling him she was equally admired in Boston &c. &c. I liked Capt. Barry very much, perhaps because he talked a good deal to me, but he really talked well and amusingly. Cousin Ben was at Aunt Mary's this evening.

Dec. 9   A dinner party at Mrs. Fitz-Uniacke's. My first. I wore my scarlet cashmere and diamonds. I forgot to say yesterday that I received a letter and basket from home by the *Halifax*. It brought me a sontag, which I wore yesterday & tonight, the blue & black satin, ribbons, laces, &c. Cousin Sarah has come home, and thinks Beppo one degree superior to Bella! The only guests at Mrs. Uniackes' were Rev. G. & Mrs. Hill & Ben Gray, besides ourselves. We had a pleasant time. Ben Gray brought a daguerreotype of Sarah & her baby to show me. It was excellent I thought. Mr. Uniacke is a very droll man. He says that from my accent and manner, one would never believe I had been in Yankee land all my life, but au contraire, that I had never left England. I am sure I am very glad and must thank dear mother for that, as well as for everything also good about me. He was very anxious when I was coming away to know if my sontag was warm enough. He was so afraid that my ears would be frost bitten. He does

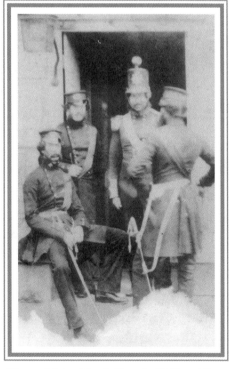

"Brevet Major Bland, Captain Tidd and Lacy of the 76th Foot Regiment at the Citadel," ca. 1855

not know how warm it is. I took a parcel to Capt. O'Brien today containing letters to mother, Josey, Morton, Molly & Mary Pope.

A bottle of lavender water for mother & a piece of striated rock for Morton, a coque de perle brooch for Mary Pope & one for Josey from Charlotte.

Dec. 10 🙼 I am very tired. I have walked around the tower & through the woods for two or three hours and then downtown shopping and calling but was very unsuccessful in both cases finding no one at home (at which I was rather pleased then other wise) and finding nothing to buy, which was better for my purse than my temper. This evening I folded and sealed Heber's reports for him. Arthur Haliburton called today with his brother Robert. I was very sorry to have missed him, as I like him very much. They make our visiting List (my own particular one) amount to (63) sixty three - quite a number for me. In the parcel from home on Thursday were some [photographs] of father. One is now hung up on the wall beside Josey's. It seems so natural! I am beginning to recover from my idle fit. I finished the eyelits in the first breadth today and Monday expect it & another. Monday eve I am to begin my studies with Heber. Latin and Spanish.

Dec. 11 🙼 Third Sunday in Advent. Heber read morning and afternoon, Uncle William preached in the morning and Mr. Hill in the afternoon. A collection was taken up for the Colonial Church and School Society. It amounted to thirteen pounds. That at St. Paul's was nineteen. And another in the evening I do not know the amount. Mr. Maturin read in the evening and Mr. Dunn preached, and such a master of bad grammar, malarkey and folly delivered with such an air assisted by the most absurdly bad pronunciation imaginable, I never listened to. It was fifty-five minutes long. I have taken a violent cold. I fear one of my regular winter ones. I only hope I shall not lose my voice. I am sorry, that if it was to come, it did not wait until after New Year's day.

Dec. 12 🙼 My cold is much worse. I have now quite a cough. Heber brought me home some cough drops, which I think did me good. Charlotte and I went downtown to day for Heber's future, though as yet unconscious edifications for tomorrow is his birthday. We got some handkerchiefs, neckties, and a gutta puncha shell for hold[ing] his cigar ashes. I got him a gutta puncha pin cushion in the shape of a [undecipherable], so that he can remove the cushion and make a little vase of it. This afternoon we called upon the Hawthorns and Solomons, thus losing the call of the Bishop. This evening I read a couple of odes from Horace with Heber and tried a few sums in Algebra. In a week or two I shall take up Spanish again. Charlie Almon came up this evening, and we all wrote Josie a round robin. Capt. Balfour wrote a note to Heber this morning and Heber gave it to me in return for folding & sealing the answer.

Dec. 13 Heber's birthday. He was much pleased with his presents. While he was at school Charlotte and I went to the gardens and got his a very pretty bouquet with a rose and some mignonette, arbutus, geraniums &c. and sent him a verse with it. He found it in his room on returning and calls now us the poetesses laureate. He bought me some paregoric sticks which have almost cured my cough.[12] I received this morning a letter from Uncle Storrs inviting me to Cornwallis at any time I chose to come. I will not go until the Spring. This noon came invitations to us (a separate one for me) for next Friday evening, from Mr. Charman, the Portuguese Consul, to celebrate the King of

Admiralty House, ca. 1865.

Admiralty House, located on Gottingen Street, was the official residence of the Commander-in-Chief of the North American and West India Station and the site of numerous parties and balls.

Portugal's birthday. We went this evening to the meeting of the Colonial Church & School Society. The speaking was wretched with the exception of Mr. Mar[ind.]'s, which was really good. Mr. Maturin's was pretty good but I was dreadfully tired, but I got laughing so that I did not know what to do. Heber sat next to me and Bella, Charlie Almon and Robert Haliburton (wish it had been Arthur) behind us. Mr. Dunn [al]most set us into convulsions, we laughed so. I never did hear a man rise and pretend to make a speech who united such bad grammar, false rhetoric and horrible pronunciation all joined together by such a delivery and such an insufferable expression of compensatory and self-conceite as I never met before.

Dec. 14   Answered Uncle Storr's letter but have not posted it yet. Accepted Miss Charman's invitation. Cousin Ben came up today to ask me to enclose a parcel for Uncle Howard the next time I send. I went walking with Heber as far as the Admiralty House over Citadel Hill, and coming back through Artillery Park we met Mr. Balfour in Col. Savage's carriage. He is indeed very handsome and my curiosity is at last gratified. I had heard so much of him, and had seen the back of his head so often that I really longed to see him. A great many visits this afternoon.

Dec. 15   I received an answer from Uncle Morton at last. Much to my regret, he cannot have me go to his house as he has not a room (that is a spare room) finished, but to make amends for that he says he is coming to Halifax to see me as soon as ever he can. I can't help thinking his bachelor ways will be broken in upon by such a novelty as a girl in his house, though I don't acknowledge it. I received today two copies of father's Mattrpan poem. I have begun Cicero's orations with Heber for prose and Horace for poetry. I have been shopping and calling all day. I bought some stays, ribbon (for Josey), net, Perfumes &c. I have been making a net skirt to wear tomorrow evening under my white tarlatan.

Dec. 16   I was all day finishing my dress to wear tonight and finally succeeded, unexpectedly to my entire satisfaction. I wore white tarlatan, double skirt, with a net underskirt, diamonds and blue shoulder knots and my embroidered shirt, the one like Bella's. We had a very pleasant evening, and did not come home before two. I do not know how much later. I danced three

Bishop Hibbert Binney, ca. 1855

*Hibbert Binney was born to an influential and wealthy
Nova Scotian family in 1819.
In 1851 he was appointed bishop, replacing Bishop John
Inglis. In 1855, he married Mary Bliss, also a member of
an influential family, and the affluent couple became well
known to Haligonians and Annapolis Valley residents
alike. Binney died in 1887 in New York City.*

sets of quadrilles, one with Dr. Grigor, one with Mr. Murphy, and one with a Mr. Forman. I liked him least of all, and I played for one set and Capt. Shellion stood by the piano beating time all the while. He did when Emily Wainwright was playing too. He is considered the handsomest man in the regiment. He is the handsomest of the Line that I have seen yet and very pleasant looking. The guests were Miss Savage, the Misses Sawyer, the Misses Bliss, the Misses Bullock, Mrs. Twining, Mrs. Taylor, Mrs. Thompson, Cassie Twining, The Misses Wainwright, and myself. The Hon. Glastonbury Neville, Hon. Hay, Capt. Newton, Capt. Shellion, Drs. Grigor Jr. & Sr., Mr. Thompson, Mr. Murphy, Mr. Truman, Mr. Cothorpe, Campbell, Capt. Bowen, and one or two others whose names I do not know. Mrs. Twining, Mrs. Taylor & Emily Wainwright sang and Cassie Twining, Mrs. Thompson, Emily & Helen Wainwright and I played. When we came away, Mrs. Thompson, the only lady remaining, for six of us went away together, was playing a reel and the gentlemen were dancing.

Dec. 17   Today the candidates for ordination are coming to dine and the Lord Bishop is to join us at tea. I will save the minutes until they come. "Saving the minutes" is what they used to laugh at me for doing at Cambridge last summer. Oh dear! I wonder if I shall ever go to Cambridge again, as I used to. I have been helping Charlotte make pudding and cake and turkey stuffing. Mr. Kinnear came to see the house while we were up to our elbows in baking and we dashed into the scullery and held the door, but after waiting about three quarters of an hour, we ventured forth to see how near he was, and found that he had gone without coming down stairs. Dear me, there is the bell. I must finish by and by.

Night. They are gone at last, it is almost eleven o'clock. The Lord Bishop came in full costume, and was pleased to admire the rooms very much. I like Mr. Griffiths very well, but Mr. Yewens is very stupid, ugly and awkward.[13] Mr. Jarvis sent an apology. I wore my scarlet cashmere. His Lordship wished to know if I had a prejudice against English Prayerbooks, thinking I was a Yankee, and seeing Heber's Prayer Book that mother gave him with father's name printed upon it. Mr. Griffiths is to preach at St. Luke's tomorrow, and Uncle William is to preach the ordination sermon. I like the bishop very much. He is much more agreeable in private that in public, that is as far as I have yet been able to judge.

Dec. 18   What a storm. It rained so hard in the night

that it woke me up and I realized the "pelting of the pitiless storm" coming home from church this morning. Heber had the whole church to himself. It is only the second time I have heard him preach. Charlie Almon offered his services to shelter me home under his umbrella, and it was the hardest work he has had for a long time I fancy. Twice we slipped, blinded by the rain in our faces, down some gullys worn into the street and we were fairly drenched. He went back for Miriam and again for Tory, but just as they started, the umbrella turned inside out, and his benevolent designs were there by parted. We were so wet. Young Wainwright was escorting Louisa home and the wind took his umbrella and blew him fairly out of the field leaving Louisa to shift for herself. Fortunately, she was very nearly home. In the Venite this morning the organ stopped suddenly and we had to finish the chant without. I rather liked the sound of it, if there had only been some gentleman to sustain it but there were only Emily Wainwright, Louisa and I. I rather liked Mr. Griffiths, but his sermon seemed rather poor compared to Heber's this morning. I think Heber is very eloquent indeed. I hope that I shall receive some letter soon. The *Halifax* ought to be in soon. I have not heard for ten days with the exception of the poem last Thursday and that gave no direct news from home. I did not go to church this evening as it stormed.

Dec. 19   We have begun to trim the church. There was very little help today. Louisa made seven wreaths. I don't know how she can work so fast. They all laughed at Dr. Grigor and me, because we made such large heavy wreaths we were wreathing together and ours are about three times the size of any others, but they'll do for something. I am dreadful tired. Received a letter from home by the *Belle* telling me to answer Richard's letter myself by the next steamer which goes Thursday. I did so accordingly. He will receive it just in time to spoil his Christmas.

Dec. 20   Still trimming the church. Capt. Barry has come and it is a pleasure to see him work, he is so graceful and agile. He has the smallest foot I ever saw for a gentleman. Much smaller than mine. His hand is too very small and well shaped but not equal to his foot. He had some Lady's boots on. He enters heart and soul into the business. Tomorrow I am to come out at General Gov's. Aunt Mary has given me my Christmas box before hand, in order to wear there. Some beautiful ribbons.

Dec. 20   I did not stay long at church for fear of being

tired out before evening. I wore a white tartlan (double skirt) with white net under it my worked skirt & my scalloped one that Mrs. Bond gave me, Aunt Mary's shoulder knots, the slippers Mrs. Caines gave me, lisle thread stocking with silk stocking under them as the night is bitter cold, pearl earrings and bracelets and feather flowers in my hair and my best handkerchief. I danced but three times, and there were but four quadrilles danced during the evening. The rest of the seventeen dances being polkas, gallops and waltzes. I danced the first quadrille with Capt. Barry, who engaged me for it as soon as I entered the room. Dr. Grigor engaged me for the third quadrille (the twelfth dance) and Charlie Almon came up when the second was forming, and asked me, but the set was full. I danced the other quadrille with Lieutenant Cothorpe of the Highlanders, Lieuts. Martin & Cothorpe & Jones asked for Polkas & Gallops as did Arthur & Robert Haliburton.

Arthur Haliburton introduced me to his sister Mrs. Cunard, as her own as a request. One or two others, asked me to polkas, but I declined. The supper was both elegant and abundant. The band played. We came home about two o'clock or a little after. I was invited the same evening to Mrs. McNab's, but could not go in consequence of being engaged at the General's. I enjoyed it very much indeed.

Arthur Haliburton, ca. 1873. Arthur, born in 1832, was the youngest son of T.C. Halburton. He married Marrianna Clay and became a lawyer.

Dec. 22

Had a letter by post, nearly a duplicate of the one by the *Belle*, to tell me to answer the Cambridge letter. It was written before the other, but they wrote by the *Belle* too, as there was a boat which would reach me first. I am glad they wrote by the *Belle* as the steamer went out today just as I received the letter by post and it would have been too

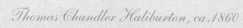

Thomas Chandler Haliburton, ca. 1860

Thomas Chandler Haliburton was a famous Nova Scotian politician, judge, and writer. He was a graduate of King's Academy and King's College, Windsor, studied law, was a judge of the Inferior Court of Common Pleas, and published numerous literary works, "The Clockmaker" being his most well-known. Haliburton first married Louisa Neville; the couple had eleven children and resided at Clifton, Haliburton's estate in Windsor. Louisa died in 1841, and Haliburton married Sarah Harriet Owen in 1856. The couple removed to England, where Haliburton died in 1865.

Laura Haliburton Cunard, ca. 1880. Laura was the daughter of T.C. and Louisa Haliburton and married William Cunard, son of Sir Samuel Cunard, Halifax shipping giant.

Louisa Neville Haliburton, 1836, photograph of a portrait by William Valentine. Louisa was the first wife of T.C. Haliburton and mother of the eleven Haliburton children. She died in 1841.

late. Still trimming the church. The choir came up this evening to practice.

Dec. 23 Received a letter from Uncle Morton this morning enclosing six pounds for a Christmas box which I was very glad to receive. This afternoon I received a letter from Miss J'ebton dated Florence where she and Mrs. Parker are spending the winter, while professor J'ebton and Mr. Parker made the tour of Greece. Charlotte, Heber, and I went downtown this evening to buy some Christmas presents for the girls. Coming home we were caught in the rain and got a complete drenching. Mr. Jones came today to spend Christmas and New Year's with us; he will probably stay several weeks.

Dec. 24 I received a letter from Mary Farish this morning, enclosing one to Aunt Mary and one to Bella. We have at last finished trimming the church, at five o'clock this afternoon. We have received an invitation to the Uniacke's next Thursday and another to an "At Home" at Government House on Twelfth Night. It is on Twelfth Night that the ring is drawn for. I wish I could get it. It is worth ten dollars and whoever draws it opens the ball with The Governor. I never have any luck as it is called, in such things, but I should like to, if only as a sort of thing to talk about, when I go home. The Christmas boxes were given out today, as tomorrow is Sunday. Mine, besides the shoulder ribbons and belt, and the six pounds from Uncle Morton, were a papeteur from Heber and a neck ribbon from Aunt Mary a very pretty one, and Charlotte had one exactly like it, which made it doubly welcome, and also a pretty little almanac and one that had the signals in it as that I can tell when my letters are coming in. I wonder if they will send me Christmas presents by the *Halifax*. I hardly expect it, as so many things were given me before I came. I gave Uncle William a book of blotting paper, Aunt Mary a bottle of Lavender, Charlotte a bottle of mignonette, Louisa a papeteur like the one Heber gave me, only mine was a little longer. [I gave] Miriam some velvet bracelets, Heber Laurt's "Essays of Elia", Bella and Tory collars and the three boys neck ties. I must stop now to write to Mary Farish.

Dec. 25 Christmas day. The first I ever spent away from home. How I should like to see them all, I know they are thinking of me, as much as I am of them. We went to St. Luke's morning and afternoon and to St. Paul's in the evening. The trimming at St. Paul's is positively ludicrous. There is a large twig or branch, fastened at every corner of every pew, and a little branch at every pillar or capital and on every gas line. I was most dreadfully tired. Charlie Almon came home with us, and staid to tea. I like him very well indeed and it is too bad to plague him as we do by talking of Josey's admirers. Poor boy! He looks the picture of despair sometimes, when we talk of it. It was a most beautiful day, but the first time I ever saw a "Green Christmas." As Lilly Allison said, it was strange to come from Boston to Halifax to see one but it was a clear, cold day and very unpleasant.

St. Paul's Church, trimmed for Christmas, ca. 1886-1892

Dec. 26 I went to church this morning being St. Stephen's day and afterwards Miriam and Heber and I went to walk. We went down by Steele's pond, and then struck through the woods.[14] We were very tired but enjoyed it very much. We saw some beautiful places and brought home some pretty greens. We saw a great many trees blown down by the wind in the storm the other day. Capt. Barry said the force of the wind was forty four pounds to the square foot. A hurricane is estimated at forty pounds. I am very anxious about the

Halifax which ought to be in by this time. Mr. Sawyer's chimney fell through the roof, causing about fifty pounds damage. There are two brigantines signaled. I hope the *Halifax* is one. Charlie is quite sick tonight. Uncle William is afraid he will have a fever. I hope not.

Dec. 27

Charlie is almost well. The *Halifax* is in. Capt. O'Brien is noted for always just escaping the storms. He started just as the last dreadful storm was over and arrived last night, just as another bad storm commenced. It snowed hard last night. Heber asked him how he spent Christmas day. He said it was the happiest Christmas he ever remembered. He passed it in saving six people form a wreck in the Bay of Fundy. They were almost exhausted when he took them off. He said it was the proudest moment of his life. I cannot have my letters until tomorrow as on account of the storm. Everything is in such confusion. Capt. O'Brien passed four vessels upside down about sixty miles out. I have bought him a scarf for a Christmas box and am going to send a couple of collars to his daughters.

Dec. 28

Innocent's Day. Went to church, then downtown to shop. Met Heber bringing up my letter, and a great big bundle is too. It had a large music book, a pair of shoes & stockings, velvet raw silk for my New Year's dress. It is just in time for Miss Morrisey comes tomorrow. We are invited to Mrs. A Uniacke tomorrow evening, and my dress out to be mended, but it is not yet [ready], and I do not know when it will be. I went down town again this evening and slipped on the ice which has

Charles Bullock, ca. 1870 Charles Beverly Bullock was the son of Rev. William and Mary Bullock. At the time of Sarah's visit he was just a boy. As an adult, he became a lawyer and member of a successful Halifax firm.

Interior of St. Luke's Church, ca. 1890.

St. Luke's Church was located on the corner of Church and Morris streets. Built by William Cogswell in 1848 as a chapel of ease to bustling St Paul's, it was made the parish cathedral in 1861 (a status previously held by St. Paul's) by Bishop Binney.
William Bullock was appointed its first rector in 1858, then dean, a position he held until his death in 1874.
St. Luke's was destroyed by fire in 1905.

given me a very bad head ache, besides smashing my bonnet. With my other letters I received another from Richard, who was very anxious at not having received my answer to his first letter. Poor fellow! He received it about Christmas. However I answered it and sent it to mother for approval. I do so wish it has never happened. I made up my parcel last night to go by the Halifax on Friday.

Dec. 29   Sewed all day with Miss Morrisey. She finished Miriam's New Year's dress and got mine and Bella's well begun. Louisa mended my dress for me and Bella fixed over one of Louisa's for herself to wear. Charlotte went too. It was so provoking. Mr. Balfour came to spend the evening and we had to go out. It was too bad when I had wanted so much to see him. But we saw him for a minute, while we were waiting for the carriage, for it stormed so that we had to ride. Fortunately it cleared up before we started, but the streets were in a dreadful condition and the wind blew furiously. The man had to walk beside the carriage at the corners, and any other particularly bad places in the roads.

I wore the same white tarlatan, pearls, and white flowers in my hair, which curled very well. We were the first arrivals (as the carriage could not come at all unless it came early) but Mrs. N. Uniacke, Miss de Le Dunier, & Mrs. Jefferys came before we entered the drawing room and very soon others came. Pretty soon the dinner party (only gentlemen) broke up and the gentlemen entered the drawing room. The Lord Bishop was there. I was introduced to Chief Justice Halliburton, Colonel Bazalgette, & Mr. James Uniacke. When the dancing began Mrs. Uniacke brought her son Robie to me to dance. The next quadrille I danced with that Mr. Forman and the next I did not dance at all. Mr. Martin asked me to polka or galop, but when I declined, asked for the next quadrille. I agreed and he talked a while until Andrew Uniacke came to take me into supper. Mr. Parsons actually brought Charlotte into supper and took away my breath. The pretense of handing me an ice, gave him an opportunity of forming an acquaintance without a formal introduction, and of telling me that "he had had the happiness of knowing my sister, summer before last" &c. &c. I was quite astounded at "Shadow" as the other officers call him, speaking to anyone but Mrs. Dick. Cousin Ben wanted me to dance the next quadrille but I was engaged to Mr. Martin and so he asked for the next and I assented, but we only danced that one, so I danced the Roger de Coverly with him. I lost a piece of my pearl bracelet and set him to work to look for it. Bella

St. Paul's Chancel, ca.1856

*Elizabeth Mary Uniacke,
ca. 1865.
Elizabeth was married to
Andrew Mitchell Uniacke;
their son was Robie Uniacke.*

set Mr. Parsons to look for it, and the unfortunate man hunted under chairs and tables &c. in vain, in the search. In the dearth of the carriages we had to wait to the last and Capt. Gore, Cousin Ben, Mrs. N. Uniacke, Mrs. Jeffrey's, Miss de Le Dunier and Charlotte, Bella & I went in and finished the supper. Capt. Gore asked me to go in to supper with him, in the middle of the evening, but I had already been. We were dreadfully frightened coming home, for fear of an upset, but the man drove very carefully, and walked beside the horse nearly all the way. A skylight was blown from the roof of a house, and dashed against the carriage wheels. It was fortunate it did not come into the carriage itself. When we got home we found that Mr. Balfour had only just gone and after he started, came back with out his hat, his hair all blown about over his face, and looking, they said handsomer than ever. He had slipped on the ice, the wind had blown away his hat, as well as blown him down and he had returned to borrow another. If we had only come home a little sooner!

Dec. 30   Miss Morrisey all day. Capt. Barry came up at one o'clock to put up the papers with the Prayer and the Creed in the church, before New Years. My dress is finished, and they say, looks very well. The wind was so high last night, that Capt. O'Brien had to put out to sea. His anchors would not keep the brig't from dashing against the wharf & other shipping near her.

Dec. 31   Very stormy indeed. I was disappointed as I wanted to go down town to get some edging for my dress. Louisa braved the weather and got it for me. I tried on the shoes mother sent me, and they do fit beautifully. I shall wear them New Year's Day. That is Monday. I read five odes of Horace with Heber and read and talked a little German with Mr. Jones. I hemmed Heber's cassock and Capt. O'Brien's scarf. I hope the weather will be fair enough to take it to him before he goes.

Fancy Dress Ball, 1883 (see p.45)
It was tradition for the governor and leading military officials to host parties and balls, especially during the holiday season. This fancy dress ball, where guests came in costume, was hosted by the Commander of His Majesty's forces at Maplewood on the North West Arm.

Halifax 1854

Jan. 1   What an opening for the young Year. Silver rain all the morning, (I hope that at least the fortune is good, that is as far as the silver goes) and real rain all the afternoon, by way of improving the walking. They said I opened the year with a conquest, because Jim Twining escorted me home with an umbrella as it was raining so hard, but behold, before we were half way home, his umbrella turned inside out. He said he only grieved for my sake as he did not mind the storm.

Jan. 2   The first time I ever spent New Year's Day in this manner before. By one o'clock we were dressed and in the parlor. The first ring was Dr. DeWolfe and after a little while they came pouring in, often ten, sometimes twenty in the room at a time. The whole number through the day was one hundred and forty. Among others the mayor, who asked us down this evening. A very quiet party but very pleasant. For the visiting I wore my raw silk (as did Bella) with the high waist, lace stomacher, and sleeves, bracelets, diamonds brooch & earrings. I enjoyed it very much indeed. In the evening I wore the low waist, and a cross, round my neck. It was a kind of musical party. I sang and played & Louisa, and Miss. H. Tremaine. The Misses Pyke, Mr. Pryor, Mr. R. Halliburton, and one or two others. I enjoyed it exceedingly though I was very tired. Mr. Duport accompanied us home, and Ben Gray came with Miriam from Mr. A. Uniacke's, where I was also invited but was already engaged to Mr. Pryor's.

Jan. 3   Feel very tired. Almost too tired to write. Only a few visits to day. Uncle William went to Mr. Stewarts (the Master of the Rolls) to dinner and met Mr. Balfour and the Walkers and one or two others. I wish I knew Mr. Balfour better. I like him very much. Have been copying the list of callers yesterday and writing home and reading German to Mr. Jones.

Jan. 4   I have done hardly anything all day, I am so tired. New Year's day is very pleasant while it lasts and to remem-

New Year's List ~ 1854.

1 Maj: Gen. Gore.
2. Maj: Ansell (retired)
3. Maj: Walford
4. Col. Bazalgette. ×
5. Col. Fraser ×
6. Col. Savage.
7. Capt. Barry × R.E.
8. Capt. Gore — × 74th
9. Capt. Newton × R.A.
10. Capt. Charnley ×
11. Capt. Dick R.A.
12. Capt. Tydd 72° ×
13. Capt. Dennis 72° × *Maj*
14. Mr. Walker × R.E.
15. Mr. Parsons × R.E.
16. Mr. Balfour × R.A. ×
17. Mr. Martin × R.A. ×
18. Hon G. Neville R.A.
19. Dr. D'Aussauville × R.A.
20. Dr. Donald R.A.
21. Dr. Jarvis R.N.
22. Dr. Gregor †
23. Dr. Jennings
24. Mr. Colquhoun × (Commissar
25. Mr. Wybault. (Commissari
26. Mr. Harvey (Ordinance
27. Mr. De Vries (Ordinance
28. Mr. Marven (Ordinance
29. Mr. Ick × (Columbi
30. Mr. Harvey × (Columbie
31. Mr. Booth. (Commissariat
32. Honble E. Collins.
33. Vernon Jones R.N.
34. Honble — Kenney.
35. The Master *Stewart* of the Rolls
36 The Mayor. *Pryor*
37 The Archdeacon. *willis*
38 Dr. Gilpin.
39 Rev. A. Gilpin
40 Rev. E. Maturin.

41. Mr Webster 72d   63. Mr A. Scott.
42. Mr Stephens. Barrack Master. 64. Mr Hare.
43. Mr J. Allison +   65. Mr E. Fairbanks.
44. Mr B. Collins x   66. Mr Creighton.
45. Mr Kinnear x   67. Mr Fay.
46. Mr DuPort. x   68. Mr A. Creighton
47. Mr B. Gray. x   69. Mr Brown x
48. Mr J. Bazalgette.   70. Mr N. Ritchie.
49. Mr Woodgate. P.O. x   71. Mr J. Grigor.
50. Mr R. Halliburton.   72. Mr Binney.
51. Mr A. Uniacke   73. Mr Taylor.
52. Mr Chipman. x   74. Mr Scott. Tremaine x
53. Mr Sawyer. x   75. Mr Hamilton
54. Mr C. Allison x   76. Hon J.B. Bland

     96. Mr Lordly.   118. Mr R. Uniacke
     97. Mr D. Allison.   119. Mr A. Uniacke Jr
     98. Mr D. Harris.   120. Mr N. Uniacke
     99. Mr Campbell   121. Mr C. Kinnear
    100. Mr Allan   122. Mr — Mose.
    101. Mr W. Silver   123. Mr W. Wainwright
    102. Mr C. Silver   124. Mr J. Moren Jr
    103. Mr Carman Jr   125. Mr C. Uniacke
    104. Mr James.   126. Mr G. Allison
    105. Mr Johnston.   127. Mr M. Moren

ber too, but it is dreadfully tiresome. I went down town to buy some finery for Government House, I got such a pretty wreath and bunch of roses for my bosom, satin ribbon for the dress and a belt &c. &c.

Jan. 5 ❦ Thursday. Miss Morrisey was here today to make my muslin dress for Government House tomorrow. Aunt Mary and all the rest think that the way I wear my hair is very unbecoming so I am to have my hair flattened tonight at Mrs. Moren's to try the effect and if it is good I will wear it to Government House tomorrow. As it is to be the only "At Home" at the House for the season, it will be very large and there will be no ring. We are going with the Chipman's.

We had a very nice time at Mrs. Moren's. My hair was liked very much so I will wear it so tomorrow. I danced with Ben, Gray, Charlie Almon, T. Grigor, P. McNab, Charlie Almon again, and was engaged to Mr. Ich & Mr. Martin, but there were not dances enough. Charlie Almon is going to take a pencil to Government House tomorrow for me to write down the names of my dancing partners as I forgot this evening once I was engaged to him. He has engaged me for the second quadrille tomorrow evening.

Jan. 6 ❦ Twelfth night. I was so tired that I had to lie down this afternoon so as to be able to go to Government House tonight. My dress will be Indian muslin double skirt with three rows of narrow satin ribbon on each skirt, breadth of crepe and ribbon flowers in my bosom and a very pretty wreath in my hair which will be braided behind and curled in front. Miriam braids hair very beautifully. She and I are the only ones going. Heber has brought us each a very lovely bouquet. Mine has the prettiest rosette imaginable in it.

Jan. 7th ❦ I did enjoy myself so much last night. We had to ride on account of the bad weather. V. Jones came up to see if we wanted an escort, but as we rode we did not require one. I had the misfortune to tear my right hand glove in putting it on. I danced every quadrille and was engaged for six more, when the ball broke up. Mr. Ridley (a very pleasant man) said we should not go alone and rode up with us. C. Almon, to whom I was engaged for the second quadrille, brought the pencil according to promise, but there were no cards given out, so it was of no use as I have no tablets, but he said as long "As long as it was brought on purpose for your use, will you not accept it?" It was a very pretty one, set with turquoises and a blood stone in the top, beautifully arranged. I am afraid he did not like it that I declined, but what could I do! If he offers it again, I shall take it, for it will show that he really wants me to take it. I think he probably bought it on purpose. It is very pretty. All through the evening I was engaged five dances ahead and if I danced the fast dances I should not be able to sit down once during the evening. Capt. Gore, Mr. Ridley, Mr. DuPort, Mr. Almon, and many others asked me, but I declined. My wreath was admired by several. It was very simple and unpretending, being little fine green feathery sprays and tiny pink and white flowers, but very elegant and suited to the shaped of my head. They say I looked very well. I hope so. My hair was braided. I have been calling today.

Jan. 8   First Sunday after Epiphany. Cold and snowy. Poor Heber had to go to Falkland and when he got there, there was no fire. He came home almost stiff with cold. I did not go to church this evening. I stayed at home to write. Uncle William has a headache coming on.

Jan. 9   I have been really industrious to day. I have made a whole breadth of eyelits. It is something quite wonderful for me. I look back upon all I did last winter and this last autumn just before I came, with a sort of wonderment at my own achievements. I don't believe I could do so much now, even if I felt like it, and tried hard. I am really ashamed of my own indolence. I intended to do so much. I thought that I would turn over a new leaf on the New Year, and here it is the ninth and I have hardly looked at a needle except when Miss. Morrisey was here. I wrote to Mrs. Caines and Isabelle Williams today and copied a collar pattern from the Ladies Newspaper.

Uncle William is very sick today, but he had to go out to see a sick person and Heber had to go to a funeral, Mr. Richardson, the father of Mr. Kinnear. The Archdeacon performed the service.

Jan. 10   The *Belle* came in today and Heber went down to see if there were any letters for me on board and found Capt. Meagher in too much in a hurry to give them to him, so he went again while Aunt Mary, Uncle William, Louisa and I went to call upon Lady Le Marchant. She was not at home, and we went next to Mrs. Noble's and then to Mr. Mulholland's. Then we went

"Luncheon at the Mess Hall
on the Day of the Sham fight,"
Emma Haliburton, 1844

The military social events attended by Sarah
were much like this, a luncheon in honour of
a mock battle, hosted at the Mess Hall,
Artillery Park. The figures in the painting no
doubt include some of the artist's sisters, who
were Sarah's contemporaries.

"Falkland Village," unknown artist, 1846

The village of Falkland is now known
as Fergusons Cove, near Purcells Cove.
The church in the center of the image is
the small chapel visited by William and
Heber Bullock. The chapel was built in
1846, and stood until the turn of the
century when it was dismantled and
rebuilt in Purcells Cove.

through Artillery Park into Granville St. Aunt Mary and Uncle William are leaving us to go to a district meeting. We met Charlotte, and went around shopping awhile, and returned home just in time to meet Heber on the way with my parcel in his hand. They write word that dear little Beppo has two teeth and has been vaccinated. Poor little thing! Mother and Father sent me a very pretty scarf for a Christmas box, Josey and Molly a steel bracelet each. Father, Mother and Morton wrote. I am so glad to receive the letters. They had not mentioned poor little Beppo before and I was afraid he was sick and they did not like to make me anxious by telling me about it. I am so glad he is not.

Jan 11 ⌇ Mrs. Uniacke's party comes off this evening. Miriam and I are the only ones going. I tore my dress terribly at Government House the other evening and never discovered it until yesterday, and I have been hard at work, with Charlotte's help to mend it. Fortunately it comes under the upper skirt, and therefore does not show. Ben Gray came in with Mr. Taylor. He is not polite at all, he kept his hat on until he was half across the room and then, seemed to take it off by accident. He affects a very rough, ungentlemanly manner, totally different from what he was when he stayed with us, some time ago. Sometimes too, he is very kind and obliging and that makes me all the more sorry when he thinks it pretty to behave so rudely. It is a shame when he might make it so pleasant for me. I feel really uncomfortable when he comes to the house for fear he may show some disrespect to Aunt Mary or do or say something disagreeable. He did not stay very long. Mrs. Fitz-Uniacke was here for a few minutes too. Charlie Almon came a little later, and we had a pleasant time talking and laughing. If Cousin Ben were only so gentle and unaffected as Charlie Almon, I should like him very much.

Jan. 12 ⌇ Uncle William's birthday. His presents, in opposition to the rule that presents should never be useful, were a hat and some bands. We did not get home from Mrs. N. Uniacke's until nearly three o'clock this morning. W. Grigor and Mather Almon came home with us. I danced every quadrille viz. with John Mills, Jack Grigor, Mather Almon, Robie Uniacke, Mr. Martin, and Mather Almon again. I enjoyed it exceedingly, only for Ben Gray's rudeness. He was as cross as a bear the whole evening. I refused to dance with him, as he asked me in such a way.

I like Mather Almon in a ball-room, he keeps me amused all

the time. I split my right hand glove again, but this time I took the precaution to take two pair. When I tore it, Mrs. Dick was putting hers on. She pulled them off immediately, and offered them to me, for she said, "you are young and dance and care about it, and I do not." It was so very kind of her. It has been raining today and I have been writing home, such a parcel of letters.

Jan. 13 🌿 Began "Sir Charles Grandison," upon Heber's recommendation, backed by Aunt Mary's approval. Have not done much of anything. The choir practice was this evening, but only Emily Wainwright and Dr. Grigor came.

Jan. 14 🌿 I have been sewing all day long. Partly on my skirt, partly darning stockings. Mr. Balfour called today, but Miriam and I were sitting up in our own room, and we should have missed his visit, for we did not hear the bell ring, and did not know any stranger was in the house, if I had not happened to go down for a book I wanted. I have missed all his former visits, by being downtown or visiting. Some of my visits have been due for a long time, I ought to return them. It is the middle of Jan. and Miriam and I have been sewing and writing up in our room, all day, without a fire, and have not felt cold at all. And in the parlor there is only the pretense of a fire, to look comfortable. Mr. & Mrs. Mulholland also called. Heber threatens me with some Damocletian sword which is to fall on my devoted head sometime next week, as soon as the hair breaks.[15] He won't tell me what it is, but says Aunt Mary has some hand in it. That being the case, I may rest easy, for she would not do anything very dreadful. Mr. Jones left us today. He has been here three weeks and a day. He intends to go to church tomorrow afternoon for the first time. He has been afraid to go before, as he might not be strong enough to stay the whole service. As it is he will sit in the gallery for fear he should not be able to stay all the time and he could leave the church more quietly than if he sat down stairs.

Jan. 15 🌿 Second Sunday after Epiphany. Heber read prayers, The Bishop preached and read part of the Aute Communions Service, Uncle William reading the rest. The three united in the Administration of the Holy Communion. I am disappointed, rather, in the Bishop. His sermon in the morning has no more to be compared to Heber's this afternoon than Wordsworth to Milton. He has such a cold, hard delivery. No

Royal Artillery Mess, ca. 1870

Royal Artillery Park, ca. 1870

Royal Artillery Park is located at the foot of the southern side of Citadel Hill. It was constructed at the turn of the nineteenth century as a residence for the Commander of Royal Engineers, who at this time was Lt. Col. Savage.

A particularly busy place and the site of grand balls and parties, Sarah often passed through the grounds while out shopping or visiting.

warmth no eloquence such as Heber has to a very great degree and I do not like his reading either. How beautifully Bishop Eastburn reads, the lessons especially. The church was very full this afternoon. Fuller Uncle William says, that it has ever been, since it was consecrated. The day is quite cold, so different from yesterday. Heber, Bella and Tory have gone to St. Paul's this evening. I have not been lately as the gas hurts my eyes so much, and I don't think it does me much good, when I am wishing all the time, that it was over. I wish Heber would preach oftener.

Jan. 16   We went to Mrs. Gardiner's this evening. I wore my raw silk. We did not want to go as we were very uncertain as to what kind of people we should meet there but we could not help ourselves. They are vulgar people and the party itself was very second-rate. The supper was nice enough, but I was pestered by a disagreeable Dr. Allen, who thought he honored me by his notice and amused by his vulgar wit in spite of all Dr. Grigor's kind endeavors to release me and get him away. We were the first to come home, which we did immediately after supper.

Jan. 17   Such a different evening from yesterday. We spent the day (a pretty cold one) shopping and calling, the evening at Miss Grove's, only Lilly Allison, Bessie and Rebecca Rand, Miriam, Bella and I were there to tea.[16] Charlie Allison and Heber came in afterwards. We had such a pleasant evening. I would give a great deal to be able to draw and paint like Miss Helen. Miss Grove and Miss Rand draw and paint beautiful but Miss Helen's are master pieces. They are really beautiful. She plays well too. Lilly Allison and Rebecca Rand and I played and sang a little too. The piano is a very hard one indeed to play. Cousin Ben and Mr. Hare and some one else were here to night but we were out. The *Halifax* will be in in a day or two. Called at the Mayor's, the Jones's & the Archdeacon's.

Jan. 18   Such a bitter cold day. I went out calling with Aunt Mary and Louisa, and really suffered, for the first time this winter. We called at Mrs. N. Uniacke's, Dr. Bell's, and Mrs. J. Allison.[17] I am very tired. The *Halifax* is in, but too late to get any letters tonight. I hope there are a good many. Miriam and Louisa are at Mrs. Moody's at a musical party. I thought of waiting up till they came home but I am too tired.

Jan. 19 Calling again. My visiting list amounts to eighty-six and I have not got through them all yet! Today I went with Miriam to Miss Boggs, Mrs. Widden and Mr. Corbett, and to the Twinings. We then went down town to shop and coming home we saw Mr. Martin by Duffus and Tupper's. He joined us and walked all the way home with us, but declined coming in on the ground of an engagement to an early dinner. Poor fellow! He says the mess dinner is not until half past seven and he gets half starved sometimes having to wait so long. He is going to leave Halifax, having by his father's desire effected an exchange to St. John's N. B. We are all very sorry, as he is a very nice young fellow but so bashful. It is really a pleasure to meet a diffident or bashful man. I like them a great deal better than those bold, conceited persons that one generally meets.

Silhouette of Elizabeth Gould Franklin, ca. 1834
Elizabeth Gould Franklin (1807-1874) was the daughter of James Bouteneau Franklin and the granddaughter of Lt. Gov. Michael Franklin. In 1830, she married Rev. Robert Fitz-Uniacke, rector of St. George's Church. The couple had no children.

My home letters are unsatisfactory. They have not received my letters by the *Halifax*. I hope they are not lost. Heber will go down tomorrow and see about it. I so hope the parcel is safe. I believe it had my answer to Richard's second letter in it, that went to mother for her approval. It will be very provoking if it is lost after the delay in the first one too, at which he so justly remonstrated. I hoped too, that my second letter might have, a little, softened any grief he might have felt at receiving my first. Mother says he spent Sunday (the 8th Jan.) in South Boston, but merely mentions the fact. Her silence as to particulars makes me fear that it was rather a painful visit or at least that I hardly know what I wanted to say

but I wish she had told me a little about it. Whether he took it in
good part or not, for with the esteem she knows I feel for the whole
family she must know that I feel uneasy as to the result.

Jan. 20   My letters are safe, and will go the next time
the *Halifax* does. I wrote by the steamer and so did Heber to say
they were safe and we were well. It snowed terribly today, but Bella
and I braved the storm, to take a letter to Mr. Fitz-Uniacke's that

was enclosed in my last letter from home. Returning we encountered Charlie Almon who walked home with us. I think he went up to Dutchtown on purpose to meet us as we saw Mather go into the office as we passed it. We had a very pleasant walk, but were very tired. I am dreadfully tired and was dreading having to go out to Mr. Fairbanks's, when a message came to put it off, on account of the news they had just received of Mr. C. Allison's death.[18] He had gone to Brazil for his health, and died on the passage. I am very sorry for the reason of the delay of the party, glad as I am to be able to stay at home. I did not know Mr. Allison, but all here did. Dr. Grigor came in with a picture he had just painted of Uncle William's coat of arms. He has done it very nicely. He was greatly shocked at hearing of Mr. Allison's death. It was the first he had heard of it. They had been great friends. It has snowed so much that we are in hopes of coasting tomorrow.

Jan. 21 🙠 The snow last night changed to rain and the coasting we had been hoping for is quite spoiled. I am very sorry for it. I wanted to go down town today to get a birthday present for father, but it rained and was very wet underfoot, thus Aunt Mary thought I had better not.

Jan. 22 🙠 The rain last night having made the walking as sloppy and rough as possible ceased, and during the night it froze into clear ice, retaining all the foot prints and roughness that were made yesterday and the day before. The wind also being very high, the walking was absolutely dangerous. The congregation was proportionally small, but as usual, the women mustered stronger than the men. I think in church the men are generally in a minority (except in the House of Correction where they number three times as many). This morning Heber read and the Archdeacon preached, this afternoon Uncle William read, and Mr. Maturin preached. A very long sermon upon the text "We loved because He first loved us." No one from this house went to church this evening but Uncle William and Heber.

Jan. 23 🙠 I went downtown with Charlotte this morning, thus losing my practicing hour (from ten to twelve). We met Heber down there and he went on with us. His cold is very much worse. We met Charlie Almon too who also joined us. It was so slippery that Charlotte and I were glad enough to have a gentleman apiece to help us walk straight. I got some black silk for an apron, a bottle of capers and a pair of gloves and a box of elastic bands for father's birthday present. Funny presents enough, but he will like them just as well, as if they were something worth having. The British steamer came in today, after causing much anxiety by her prolonged delay as Sara Stewart came on her. She was offered a winter in Italy and refused it. I cannot conceive of such a thing, but so it is. I made up my home parcel, and there are twelve letters, besides the capers &c.

Jan. 24   I have not been out all day. Heber took down my parcel to Capt. O'Brien, but had to give it to the steward, as the capt. was not there. Bella and Tory went out to walk with the Heads and brought back Capt. Barry. And went out again & brought back Charlie Almon. Mr. Bland was out coasting on his toboggan today and we were highly amused watching the numerous casualties that took place. Heber met Mr. Balfour downtown, and Mr. B. told him that he came to spend the evening with us last night and exerted his whole strength to open the porch door but not succeeding he concluded we were all out or not visible so he went away again. It was so provoking, so very provoking. I have never happened to be at home when he was here, and they say he is particularly agreeable when he comes to spend the evening in a sociable way. The door sticks dreadfully. Sometimes we have been obliged to go in the back way, not being able to open it.

Uncle W. has gone to the Archdeacon's to dinner. Heber was invited but was too ill to go. Miss Morrisey was here all day making Louisa a dress and is coming on Thursday to make me one to wear to Miss Black's where we are invited.

Jan. 25   Uncle William's confirmation class began today and I went to it. There were about nineteen altogether. Afterwards I went out shopping and calling with Louisa, which finished the afternoon, indeed, the whole day, as we were too tired to do anything when we came home. We bought some lace and trimmings for the dress I am to wear to Miss Black's. I must write to Uncle Morton for some money, as I almost emptied my purse today.

Jan. 26   A most violent, though light drifting, snow storm. Miss Morrisey came and made my dress beautifully. We had tickets to the opening of the House by the Governor, and went in spite of all the storm, as it was a ceremony I should not have anoth-

"Sledding on Citadel Hill," Capt. Bland, 1853.
Much like today, Citadel Hill was a favourite place for Haligonians
to toboggan in the nineteenth century.

er chance of witnessing. I was much struck with the building itself, but the ceremony was not at all impressive. There was no religious service, which, I think should be indispensable, and the whole thing amounted to nothing more than a roll call, a speech, and a dismissal. The room where we were was a very handsome one with several fine paintings in it among others portraits of several kings, queens, and magistrates. The storm cleared up about sunset, and Uncle was to come up for us at half past eight, but was long after nine when he did come. He said the drifts were so deep that he could hardly get through some of them. It was a very heavy drag for the poor horse, almost all the way up hill. The Wainwrights were going with us, but changed their minds, so Charlotte, Louisa and I went. I danced four quadrilles with Vernon Jones, one with Mr. Duport, one with Mr. Taylor, one with Mr. Black. Young De Blois wanted me to dance with him, but he did not ask in a way that pleased me, so I would not dance with him. I cannot bear him. I like him less than any one in Halifax. A piece of his meanness, even treachery and falsehood came out yesterday, that sickened me of him. Josey received a prayer book anonymously, just before she went away, and Will De Blois, meeting her, gave her to understand that it was from him, which made Josey rather undervalue it except as a memento of Halifax and last night Miriam and Charlie Almon were talking when Miriam happened to mention the Prayer Book W. de Blois gave Josey. Charlie could not restrain his indignation, and his evident surprise & dismay excited Miriam's curiosity. She cross-questioned him until he confessed that he had sent it to her, and W. de Blois had gone to see him a day or two afterwards and asked him if he had not, saying that Josey had received it and ascribed it to him, (C.A.), thus gaining the credit of it with Josey and effectually putting a stop to any inquires Charlie might have made for Charlie would not for the world, thinking that Josey knew who sent it, have pressed the assurance of it upon her. He had too much real generosity for that and it was well for his good standing with Josey that he did not as long as she knows it at last, for Josey despised W. de Blois as much, for sending a thing anonymously, and then telling her (as he did, virtually) that it was from him. She said "If he wanted me to know, why did he pretend to conceal it?" and Charlie will rise in her estimation by his delicacy and want of ostentation. "Palam qui meruit ferat."[19] I wrote to Josey as soon as I heard of it, for I did not want W. de Blois to get the credit of it a minute longer than I could help. Mean fellow.

We came home from Miss Black's about one o'clock, dreadfully tired, although we had enjoyed it very much. I received few posts, a letter from Selina Bond dated Jan. 10, R. must have received mine before that & I hope it is to intimate that it is to be as if nothing had happened.

Jan. 27 I went down town with Bella today and bought some music principally dancing music, as I have felt rather awkward for not knowing any when I have been asked to play for dancing. We met Heber downtown and Charlie Almon and they walked home with us. This afternoon Miriam and I called upon Mrs. Andrew Almon, as she intends returning to Cambridge in the next steamer. I did not think her very agreeable or polite either, for she all but turned her back upon us, the whole time we were there. She is handsome, but has very repelling, despicable manners, or rather no manners. The Rands and Lilly Allison called. Charlotte intends asking them here next Thursday with a few others, and having a small musical party.

Jan. 29 Fourth Sunday after Epiphany. The organ acted shamefully. Louisa sat on one side of Emily Wainwright and

I the other picking up the notes as she played them for there are five notes that did not sound at all, and eight which when played, stayed down, and Louisa and I had to keep picking upon Miss N. Morris, an old woman who used to know father. She is a melancholy instance of the uncertainty of worldly prosperity. She a rich, beautiful, sought-after belle, now a poor, withered wrinkled, lonely old woman.

Today was one of the coldest this winter. In the morning, about eight or nine o'clock, the thermometer was at fifteen below zero. The highest point today was three below. Uncle William has just come in from evening church with the intelligence that it is now twelve below. I have been answering Selina Bond's letter. The barber on the water was more than fifty-feet high, and completely hid the water. What is still more unusual, it has lasted (in a less degree) all day showing extreme cold. But I have felt no discomfort whatever from it, except its taking my breath away, when I went into the open air. All the others have been shivering and shaking, and cowering over the fire, while I have been quite comfortable in the farthest corner of the room.

Jan. 30 Father's birthday. I hope he received my birthday letters and parcel. I calculated that he would have them yesterday. Charlotte had a Roly Poly Pudding in honor if it. Aunt Mary, Louisa and I called at the Blands, Formans & Bazalgettes and then down town at Mrs. Hawthornes. Aunt M. called upon Mrs. Dr. Jennings, but I came home. We met a great many sleighs, among others, Capts Gore & Barry with four-in-hand, Mather Almon, the Uniackes, Gore's, Sawyers, Ich, Harvey, Almons &c. Some of our people went with Mr. Lynch to a lecture and brought Charlie Almon home with them & went out coasting. They came in afterwards and had tea. Charlie Almon looked so pale & haggard. He had been obliged to stand during the lecture in a crowded room for an hour and a half and while coasting he had met with many mishaps. Tory fell with her whole weight upon him two or three time and I believe Miriam did once which was no trifle.

Jan. 31 Mrs. Ward's birthday. It rained all day. We went to Mr. Lynch's in the evening. It was very pleasant, but so difficult to get there from the state of the roads that I for one, was quite tired out. We were nearly half an hour, going that short distance & coming home, I gave my self a terrible wrench trying to save myself from falling. Mary Bliss told us that Annie Allison died yesterday at twelve o'clock.[20]

Feb. 1   Mr. Jones came today to stay two or three months. The confirmation class met for the second time and has increased to more than twenty. Mrs. Major brought her two daughters, and had to wait for her carriage for some time afterwards. And having traveled in many parts of the world, gifted with a fine mind improved by a fine education, and habits of observation, her conversation could not but be both instructive & amusing. The choir came to practice this evening. Emily Wainwright did not come, so I played. Dr. Grigor has promised me some seals, as I am making a collection of them.

Feb. 2   Miss Morrisey all day. I sewed a good deal, practiced a little, helped Charlotte make an architectural drawing of our house for a friend of Uncle William who is going to build one like it. I drew the front elevation and have been finishing up my home letters, as there is a good chance of sending them. I wrote also to Uncle Morton and Aunt Eliza and arranged some seals Dr. Grigor sent me today. He sent me some seals too which I sent to father. Bella has a very hoarse cold and it sounds so funny. Heber has been suffering very much from his tooth. I got a box of thread to send to mother & one for myself.

Feb. 3   Bella is quite sick with her cold. She was in bed until twelve or one o'clock. Dr. Grigor came this evening to confirmation class, not knowing that it was put off. He says that the seals I have collected will be very apt to melt and become useless in warm weather. I hope they will not. I read a little German today and find that I have lost a good deal for want of practice.

Feb. 4   Bella is still quite sick. Heber went to Dr. Van Buskirk about his tooth today and he must have one taken out which is not very comfortable as his teeth are unusually firm in his head. It is very cold. Bella Hartshorne came up and invited us to tea to meet Lady Wilkins.[21] Heber & Andrew Uniacke, Charlie Gore & a Master & Miss Creighton were there too. I think Lady is very pretty. She both speaks and looks like her mother and has a most beautifully fair complexion. Charlie Gore & Andrew Uniacke walked home with us. Only Tory and I went. I like Charlie Gore. He is so amusing and has so much character for so young a boy, but with all his fun & poke, he was never rude or ungentlemanly. Mr. McGrath, who was going to take my parcel, has changed his mind and is not going till the next steamer. So Heber got it back for me, and took it down to the *Belle* which goes Monday morning.

Feb. 5 ✒ Fifth Sunday after Epiphany. We had to sing without an organ and sang only the psalms and hymns. I went to St. Paul's in the evening, but was so tired that I do not think I will go again. A man fainted in the gallery and they made such a noise getting him out. The *Arabia* could hardly get out today for the sea in the harbor. It was almost entirely frozen over, and the *Arabia* had to cut her way through it and after she had passed, the barber could be seen rising through the opening thus made. When she came in, she was so weighed down by the weight of ice collected on one side of her, that people could not walk the deck, without holding onto something, it slanted over so. I wrote to Mary Farish today.

Feb. 6 ✒ The *Belle* is frozen up, so that she could not get out this morning. I expect the *Halifax* in daily. It snowed hard this afternoon so that I could not go to Mrs. Wilkins as I promised Lady. An invitation came for Charlotte, Heber, and me, to go to Mrs. W. Lawson's Wednesday. Louisa and Miriam are gone to Mrs. Silver's this evening. Mr. Balfour is going away in May. I am so very sorry. He is the only one in Halifax I cared particularly to know, (that is besides my own relations) and I have seen less of him that of any one else. It is too bad. I am very tired to night so cannot write any more. Oh, I forgot, I began my cloak collar today.

Feb. 7 ✒ It was bitterly cold today, so Aunt Mary thought I better not go out. Mr. Balfour came in this evening quite unexpectedly, just after tea and stayed until half past twelve. I guess he liked it, for he did not half relish the thoughts of leaving our pleasant circle to go to his cold, solitary rooms where, he says, he has to read with his great coat on. The room was so dreadfully warm that Bella and I were crimson and felt so restless and uncomfortable, that we did not know what to do with ourselves. The gas would not burn, something was the matter with it, and we had such a bright fire to light the rooms and it looked so cheerful and cozy. So, Bella set Mr. Balfour to work to make her a seal and kept him at it most all the evening. He is very handsome, he looks so perfectly peaceful, his eyes look so clear, as if you could look through them, into his very soul. About ten, the gas began to burn again but it was not half so pleasant as before. We had such a nice time. Bella gave me twenty or thirty cards, among others, Mr. Balfour and Blands, and Parsons's. Received an invitation to the Artillery & Engineer's Ball.

Feb. 8   Received a letter form Uncle Morton while I was dressing, enclosing five pounds and one from Aunt Eliza, just as I was starting out to call. Capt. Tidd is very sick; we called to see how he was and Mrs. Tidd too. I got a pair of gloves at Fenerty's to see if they are any better than the others in Halifax which are, without exception, horrid. I caught a slight cold, but went with Charlotte to Mrs. Lawson's. I was dreadfully tired and did not enjoy myself at all. I had such a cold and headache. I played bagatelle with Arthur Haliburton and talked to Dr. Grigor on the stairs watching the others playing which was the pleasantest part of the evening. It snowed and drifted silently coming home, and Mrs. Lyttleton came with out escort and dragged her beautiful dress through all the drifts, ruthlessly. She had on a beautiful dove col-ored moire antique, with a magnificent black lace over dress.

Feb. 9   Such a storm! Raining, pouring, as if whole clouds were coming down bodily. The Diocesan Meeting was deferred until next Wednesday, and it after all, cleared up so beau-tifully and is such a bright moonlight. Mr. Nichols came up and got Heber to go down to some meeting or other at Mr. Gilpin's.

Feb. 10   I went down to Mrs. Wilkins's at ten o'clock and found them just at breakfast. She said she would go to both balls with me. So I am at rest upon that point. We spent this evening at Mrs. Binney's. It was very pleasant, there were some beautiful books there called "Nooks & Corners of Old England." I could have looked at them all day, all night rather.

Feb. 11   Minnie Wilkins said it was her birthday yes-terday so I went downtown with Bella and bought a little book for her at Graham's.[22] I got some music for myself at the same time. We went backwards and in[wards on] Hollis St. until I was quite ashamed trying to meet Heber, who had gone for my letters. At last we came home in despair and found him quietly eating his lunch. He had been down for my letters and could not get them for an hour so I had to wait patiently. When he did come it was with a parcel large enough to reward me for the delay. A box with papers

& letters and chocolate that I had sent for to give Uncle William.

Feb. 12 ⚭ Septuagesima Sunday. Mr. Avery preached this morning and Mr. Bliss this afternoon. Mr. Nichols read prayers this afternoon. Heber went to Falkland, and Mr. Balfour went with him. Heber said it was so slippery, that it was all they could so to get along. Mr. Balfour slipped once, and came within and inch of "spoiling his beauty" Heber said, by falling on his face but just saved himself. Heber had to perform a baptism and he said the water froze while he was performing the ceremony.

Feb. 13 ⚭ Went downtown and bought a pink dress for the Engineer's Ball, a brooch as Uncle Morton's Christmas present to me. I received the first Valentine in this house. Miriam and Heber and I went down to Steele's pond for a walk and met Capt. Dennis on our way. Heber and Miriam gave me a delightful slide only we met Mr. Martin and Mr. Marvin just as we were going to stop, and I caught my foot on a rough place, and came down on my knees just in front of them. I jumped up in such a hurry. They hardly knew I was down before I was up, talking to them.

Feb. 14 I sent my letters home today. Rec'd a note from Charlie Almon to say he had done something I asked him to and he had done beautifully too, though he did not say that. We went down to Mrs. Wilkins's to see how I was to arrange about meeting her and did a few errands for her. I went down at eight o'clock and from there Mrs. W. Sardy & I went together in Mr. Uniacke's carriage to the Ball. Andrew Uniacke came for us. Just as we reached the ball, Col. Savage's carriage came up behind us and the horses reared so, I thought they would come through our carriage any minute. Sir Gaspard was there, Lady Seymor and her daughters & son. Lady Le Marchant, Gen. & Mrs. Gore, Capt. & Minnie Gore and many others. But I will never go to another. It was so pleasant, but so mixed. Dress makers, mechanics, common soldiers &c. The best fancy dress (there were very few) in the room was Capt. Chainley's. He was dressed as a red Indian, a Newfoundland tribe, now nearly extinct. His dress was complete, even to a couple of scalps. Sir Gaspard took great notice of him and it. Young Mather Almon was dressed as an Indian of a different tribe and looked very handsome. Charlie as a Hungarian and W. De Blois as Valentine, also looked remarkably well.[23] Mr. A. Uniacke as a gentleman of the olden time, and Mr. Wainwright as

Pickwick were very good. That was almost all. There were many, very many persons I did not know or wish to, in character, but nearly all poor, or incorrect. The pleasantest part of the evening to me was the quadrille I danced with Capt. Dennis. He has been to Greece and was describing the dress, and telling me all about it. I thought the carriage would never come to take us away. My dress was in rags when I came away there was such a crush at the door to come through. Somebody's spurs caught the skirt, a coachman's whip, the tunic, and I thought I should come away minus the whole. I was introduced to Col. Murray, and danced the first quadrille with A. Uniacke opposite to Lady Le Marchant and Lady Wilkins. We came home at half past twelve. Capt. Barry wanted me to walk and let him go with me, but even if I had been willing I could not as I had only my camel's hair shawl on and my satin slippers. I expect more pleasure from the Engineer's Ball.

Feb. 15   I am more tired than I ever was before after a ball. Heber was forced, much against his will, to give a holiday for the schoolroom (which was used as the supper room, last night) was in such a condition they could not enter it. Cake, jelly, custard, meat, wine, &c &c all over the floor. When I opened my desk this afternoon, I found a letter to Josey that Heber had written last night with a Latin note to me asking to send it to her. Day before yesterday I began again my evening lessons in Horace and Spanish but have been out every evening since, so it is a rather unsteady way of studying. I find I have not forgotten so much Spanish as I expected. Tonight we went to the Diocesan meeting. Heber's was decidedly the best speech of the evening. The bishop, who had the chair, pushed away all the papers on the table, which had previously accepted a good deal of his attention, and never turned his eyes from his face. Heber was repeatedly stopped by applause, led off by the Bishop or Chief Justice. I felt proud of being his cousin. Felt glad that the people I knew, knew that I was his cousin. He is wonderfully eloquent and leaving himself so entirely out of his speech, that entranced as you were with his eloquence, you forgot the speaker, forgot the speech in the weighty matter of which it treated. So different from the Rev. Geo Hill's, who did not speak a sentence in which the great "I have spoken, Let all attend" was not the chief point dwelt upon. Mr. A. Uniacke, made a very great speech, so did the Bishop, so did the Chief Justice. I did not like the rest. I was too tired perhaps to pay attention. When we were coming home, we found that the weather had changed and the

sleet was falling so that it was almost impossible to stand. We divided off into pairs. C. Almon had been home during the meeting, and brought down a pair of creepers for Uncle William, which was a very acceptable piece of thoughtfulness. Uncle William, Louisa and the Groves went together, Miriam & Rebecca Rand & Misses Hare & Moss formed a second party. Mr. Boggs accompanied Charlotte & me and the boys. Ben Gray took Lilly [indecipherable] under his arm and C. Almon, Bella. Heber went home with Sophy Head & Mrs. Stephen Boggs, so we were pretty well scattered over the town. Our dresses were stiff with sleet and my hair glittered like spun glass.

Feb. 16　⁓⊱　I have been lying down all the morning. I was so tired walking on that slippery ice and I was going to the Almon's this evening and had to rest for it, especially as I am going out again tomorrow to the Engineer's Ball. Four days running is dreadful dissipation. Sarah Stewart was married today and Heber brought home a bundle of cake for me to send home. Spent such a pleasant evening in spite of my fatigue. Charlie Almon stuck by me the greater part of the evening. Just before supper Mather put on his Indian dress, as many of the party had not seen it. It was wonderful how singularly like an Indian he looked. Not an Indian of the present day, but as they must have been when first awakening to a sense of their powerlessness to resist the onward march of the whites, bringing civilization to the Western Hemisphere, and ruin and decay to its inhabitants. A melancholy, defiant pride in his dark eyes, and stern handsome face, and the stoic immobility of features proverbially characteristic of "the man without a tear." He had, also to perfection, the peculiar gait of the Indian favored by his figure, which was set off to great advantage by the dress which was one of the finest specimens of Indian beading I had ever seen.

Neville & Newton were there and Neville told Miriam and Miss Hartshorne, as a wonderful piece of fun, that Capt. Barry had received a valentine. Such a valentine! He had learned it for the fun and repeated it little thinking that we had seen and laughed at it before he had. Capt. Barry has shown it to everyone. I like Mrs. Almon very much. Little Anna Almon is the very counterpart of Molly, only younger and consequently smaller. But even younger in expression and movement of her features, she was remarkably [a]like. C. Almon came home with me superseding R. Haliburton who asked to, but went back for his umbrella and lost his chance.

Ben Gray walked home with Miriam and Heber with Charlotte and Louisa. We rode down. Capt. Gore was there the first time I had seen him in plain clothes. Mrs. Almon insisted upon my singing, unwilling as I was. Unfortunately, obliged to consent, I chose to sing while they were all at supper, hoping so to escape much attention; but just as I began they left the supper table and came into the room where I was. So I did not get off as easily as I expected.

Feb. 17 ❦ Aunt Mary would not let me get up until Miss Morrisey came this morning for fear I should be too tired to go out this evening. Miss Morrisey made me a pink tarlatan dress, which they said was very becoming. I wore my hair curled down on my shoulder, and a spray of roses twisted into the curls on one side. My hair curled very well. I went down to Mrs. Wilkins's and rode from her house to the place. It was in the mess room of the Artillery. I never enjoyed a ball so much since I have been in Halifax. Every thing was so elegant. The entries and ladies' rooms lined with flags, wax candles instead of gas, which is much pleasanter for the eyes. The ladies room was furnished with lounges, full length cheval glass, half length glasses, hair pins, pins, needles, &c &c. Everything that could be desired. Officers always ready in the entry to hand the ladies in, or do anything for them and Mrs. Col. Savage and Mrs. Dick received the guests. We were among the first arrivals and Mrs. Dick herself led me into the drawing room, to show me the style in which the officers did things. Mr. Martin & Mr. Parson's showed me all the curiosities, as Mrs. Dick was obliged to return and receive the other visitors. There was a splendid case of medals belonging to Mr. Walker. Card tables, books, some rare ones, pictures, some of them painted by the officers themselves, articles of bijouterie & bertiè &c. Mr. Martin said every officer contributed his choicest rarities to adorn the room. V. Jones engaged me for the first & sixth quadrilles in the morning. I danced also with M. & C. Almon, Marvin & Martin, & when I came away I was engaged to A. Haliburton, R. Duport, & Capt. Barry, Parsons, R. Haliburton & C. Gore & one or two others asked me to dance, but I was engaged. C. Almon took me to supper and there again everything was most elegant. The carriage was announced just after I went in, so I had to leave. Major Lloyd led Mrs. Wilkins & C. Almon me to bid Mrs. Savage & Mrs. Dick good night then to the carriage. I was perfectly delighted with the whole affair; it was so elegant and just as it should be. Every individual officer seemed to devote himself to making everything go off well. Mrs. Dick wanted me to stay. She said if Mrs. Wilkins insisted on going then she would be most happy to see that I was safe, and went home pleasantly but I could not leave Mrs. W. so abruptly after her kindness, neither could I keep Aunt Mary sitting up for me, so I came home.

Feb. 18 I did not get up very early, as we did not come home last night until nearly two o'clock. I went downtown with Charlotte, but we did not stay any longer than we could help as it began to snow. Minnie Wilkins is quite sick with a sore throat. Mr. Balfour called this afternoon, and was very pleasant but the boys wanted me to go down stairs a minute to help then about their composition & when I came up again, he was gone. Heber brought home "Hoods Up the Rhine." It is very amazing.

Feb. 19 Sexagesima Sunday. Sacrament Sunday. We had five clergymen this morning, viz. The Bishop, Uncle W., Heber, Mr. Nichols, & Mr. De Blois, W. de Blois's brother. Mr. de Blois read & Heber preached a very eloquent sermon on the text "Jesus Christ, the same yesterday and today and forever" Heb. 18, 8. I do wish he c'd preach oftener. He read & Uncle W. preached this afternoon. I have begun, on Heber's recommendation, to read "Wordsworth on the Apocalypse" a noble work, so far as I have yet read, being the course of Halsean Lectures for A.D. 1848. I am very much interested in it.

Feb. 20 I have read a little more in the "Apocalypse" and like it better and better every time. I went down town with Charlotte this morning and stopped at Mrs. Kinnear's to get some Shangae [sic] eggs she promised Charlotte. It was so pleasant, that I went out again with Bella in the afternoon, but it had grown very cold and was not so pleasant, so we went down town and bought some music at Graham's. We met Heber walking with Mr. Martin on our way home, so H. came home with us. Heber married a soldier named Joe Spence to Mr. Mulholland's girl named Janet McDonald I believe. Aunt Mary gave me another coin besides one I had before to send to father. I think it is a Russian coin. We are invited to Mrs. Tremain's tomorrow.

Feb. 21 It snowed (as we thought) a little, this afternoon, but it proved a good deal after dark, for on setting out to the

Tremain's we were astonished to find ourselves, after a very few slips, up to our knees if not deeper, in a snow drift, and blinded by the flying snow, which was fine and light as dust under the influence of a high wind was in our faces and white with the even fine particles. We were obliged to break the path and occupied equally with keeping our equilibrium and nice dresses, we found it no easy task. But supported by good spirits & good temper & mutual encouragement and sympathy, we arrived safely, though somewhat out of breath at Mrs. Tremain's. They live next to Mrs. Wilkins. They were disappointed by the weather of many of their expected guests, but the rooms were very comfortably full and it was perhaps pleasanter than if all had come. I wore my rosebud dress. Young Mr. Tremain & Mr. Creighton were very attentive to me and Mr. Tremain Sr. led me into supper. I sang after Louisa, and Mary Bliss after me & Robert Haliburton filled up the rest of the evening. Heber was showing me some lines in Horace the other day, when I was reading an ode to him which I thought applied beautifully to him. I believe they ran thus: "Omnibus hoc vitium [est] cantoribus inter amicos/Ut numquam inducant animum cantare rogati./Iniussi numquam disistant."[24] Someone at Mr. Almon's the other night said, while Mr. R. Haliburton was singing, "A lady will never remain at the piano with out entrealy [sic], a gentleman, once seated, will never leave it." Mary Bliss offered us a seat in her sleigh coming home which was very acceptable, as the snow was deeper than ever. Heber, Charlotte, Louisa & I were there. Young Tremain showed me two specimens of Prussiate of Potash, one red and one yellow, which he had brought from Scotland. He says there are but two establishments (in the world I think, if I remember right) where it is made. It is very heavy and the crystals are of rather peculiar shape. Something like this, on as near as I can make it as I do not know how to draw. A & B, are the points where the string is passed through, round which the crystal was formed, so that it did not form regularly round the string, though the crystal itself was so perfect as if drawn by geometrical rules. Miss Jones was married to Rev. C. Shriver today. Charlotte & Aunt Mary went.

ACADIAN SKATER'S VALSE.

VIEW ON FIRST DARTMOUTH LAKE.

FANTASIA for the PIANO FORTE.
COMPOSED and DEDICATED to the LADIES of HALIFAX by J. HOLT
BANDMASTER H.M. 2ND BATT. 17TH REGT. HALIFAX, N.S

Published by R.T. MUIR 125 Granville St.

Skating Party on the Dartmouth Lakes, ca. 1855

"English and Newfoundland
Mail Vessels in Halifax Harbour,"
George Henry Andrews, 1861

Halifax Harbour was a constant host to a
range of sailing and steam vessels.
Mail vessels were a daily concern to Sarah as
they were her only tie to her family
and friends in Boston.

Feb. 22   Letters from home. I am afraid they have missed another parcel by the *Halifax*. It will be too provoking if they have. I have sent for a piece of music, which they sent me. Beppo has another tooth coming. Mary wrote to Charlotte. Mr. Pope is much better. The *Belle* has been in since Sunday, but it was not in the paper until this morning. I do not know why. We went to Mrs. Kinnear's this evening. She had her new service of silver and china out for the first time, in honour of our coming. It has just come out to them from England. We felt quite honoured.

Feb. 23   Very rainy indeed. Bella and I went down town to take a parcel to Heber, to go by the *Belle*, and to post a letter to Uncle Morton. I want to take drawing lessons, and wrote to him to ask him about it, as he will have to give me two pounds if I do. Rec'd a letter from home by post to ask me to send back a scarf I had here & did not want, as Molly is to take the part of a flower fairy in Mr. Johnson's next concert. Mr. Johnson has been very kind to Molly indeed, and would not take her subscription when she offered it, as "he had invited her." I think she will have a very fine voice, when it is cultivated. Bella & I were drenched through when we came home. I have had the earache for the last few days, but not very severe. Tory has been very sick with it, but is very patient indeed. I, with some of the others, was vaccinated today.

Feb. 24   This being the Festival of St. Matthias, I feel bound to expatiate on the judicious arrangements of stated seasons for devolon for the man who has no particular time for reflection, is in a fair way of having none at all, so on the very lowest plea of utility. The plan is valuable; consistent and wholesome.[25] I will not be answerable for all Heber's interpolations, appropriate or inappropriate, the latter of which I think the exortium to which he has left me to furnish the Argumentum, Exemplum &c. to be.

Miss Morrisey came today to make Miriam's dress. It was a very pretty plaid, brown and blue, dark. It was very cold to day. C. Almon came in this evening and we taxed him with having sent a Valentine to Josey. He turned all sorts of colours, but could not give a flat denial. Tory is really sick with her earache.

Feb. 25   Mary and I went downtown today. I have been very seldom with her. I bought a coque de perle brooch to fasten my scarf, as I do not like to use my handsome ones for it, as it is not very safe. I got a book on architecture for Morton, as Monday week is his birthday. Heber & Mr. Balfour were out walking together this afternoon and Mr. B. fell down twice. I never knew any one tumble about as he does and yet he never wears creepers. Perhaps he wants to get accustomed to it. Not falling, but to slippery walking. The way he fell down twice coming home from the Diocesan Meeting and Heber says he does not "fall easy" either. Poor fellow!

Feb. 26   Quinquageisma Sunday. Uncle William is very sick with one of his headaches and Heber had to perform the service all alone this morning. He preached a beautiful sermon on the parable of the prodigal son. He could not get to Falkland on account of the ice. The steamer came from Bermuda today, bringing the Admiral, but not Dr. Munro, to our great sorrow, and what is worse the news that he does not now intend to come, but to proceed direct to Barbados. Mr. Balfour had to go down to tell Sir George that they could not salute him, as it was Sunday, and offered to tomorrow, which Sir George declined. In consequence of having to go as far he did not get to church until the second lesson, it being Sacrament Sunday at [the] Garrison Chapel, which kept him in late this morning. Early this morning (at eight o'clock) the thermometer was six below zero. At two in the afternoon it was thirty above, rising thirty six degrees in six hours. The bishop preached this evening but I did not go as I was tired, and the gas hurts my eyes. They say the bishop preached a splendid sermon.

Feb. 27   It s a blustering day, tho' very mild, so I did not go out. I hope to receive an answer from Uncle Morton tomorrow about the drawing lessons. Mr. Martin (B.A.) called the afternoon. It is a false report that he is ordered to Turkey. He is going to St. John N.B. next April and says he had much rather go to Turkey. I have read a couple of odes of Horace today and some Spanish with Heber. We are progressing, as the Yankees say, finely. I was reading a very interesting article today about the division of time among the ancients, by Boyd I think. I shall copy part of it to keep. Bella and Charlotte have gone to the Christian Association tonight. I thought the wind sounded very high and dec'd not go. Mr. Balfour wants to read the "Apocalypse" and as he is going away in a month or so, I told Heber I would rather wait until he has read it first and then finish it.

Built in 1844, the Garrison Chapel was located on the corner of Brunswick and Cogswell streets to accommodate the hundreds of troops stationed in the city. It was opened in 1846 and served as the official place of worship for all British soldiers in Halifax, with the exception of Presbyterians and Roman Catholics. Bullock occasionally preached there. The chapel was closed in 1905 and sold to the congregation of Trinity Church.

Feb. 28   Rec'd a letter from Uncle Morton saying to begin drawing by all means if I wish and he will provide me with whatever I wish. I intended to go and see Miss McKie today to ask her about it, but rec'd a note from Cousin Ben, to say that he would be very happy if any of us wished to go over to the Dartmouth lakes, as it was a splendid day, and the skating was excellent. So Miriam, Bella and I went & called for Charlotte Fairbanks on the way. Almost down to the ferry boat we encountered Mr. Tremain, a very pleasant person, and he went too. We met C. Almon in the boat, so we made quite a party. Mr. Ich joined us also. On the ice, Mr. Martin joined C. Fairbanks and her brother. I believe Gus Fairbanks came to us and we had a splendid time. Such nice slides. The ice was not so good as we expected but we found a beautifully smooth place after a while and enjoyed it fully.

Capt. Dennis joined us on our way home and was very interesting. He told us about Corfu and Malta where he had been stationed at different times. It was half past six when we came home. Capt. Dennis told us that the church of St. John in Malta has a door of solid silver. It had one of gold, but it was carried away by the French and the vessel it was carried in was sunk in the battle of the Nile. The floor is of marble mosaic forming the shields of the knights, who are buried there. He told me, what I did not know before, that the common people speak Maltese, which is a kind of Arabic. I thought before that Maltese was a kind of Italian or Spanish. He says the higher class speak Italian. I am dreadfully tired, but enjoyed it very much.

Coming back Cousin Ben and I had lagged behind somewhat and saw an old woman who could not get over a very slippery place on the ice. Cousin Ben immediately went up to her and bowing, asked permission to assist her and handed her over the ice as gracefully and tenderly as if she had been the highest lady in the court and then came back to me, and went on with his sentence, as if he had never interrupted it. He certainly can be most fascinating when he wishes. It is only a pity that he ever takes it into his head to act against his nature and be rude and disagreeable. When I came home I found another note from him with some seals. He has promised to try and get me some autographs for father. He had heard that Augusta Haliburton is going to marry a gentleman in England also named Haliburton.

Augusta Neville Haliburton, ca. 1880. On June 27, 1854, Sarah attended Augusta's marriage to her cousin Alexander Fauden Haliburton.

March 1   Ash Wednesday. Miriam and I are so stiff from yesterday's fatigue that we can hardly stand. I went to church three times & heard the Commination Service for the first time in my life. I did not like it at first, but in the evening, instead of the regular evening service, the Bishop ordered the Commination Service, the Litany, and the Communion Service to be read, followed by a sermon explaining and defending the Commination Service and I do not think I ever enjoyed a service so much. I never heard Uncle William preach so well or so earnestly. This morning there were only Louisa, Bella and I to sing, and without any instrument but a pitchpipe, it must have sounded rather poor and then, at least, it was very appropriate for Ash Wednesday. The church looked so bare without the trimmings.

March 2 Rec'd a note from cousin Ben asking Uncle Howard's address. It was the first intimation I had received of the their return from Manchester. Charlotte and I went downtown this afternoon to get my drawing materials. Met Cousin Ben down there and he walked up with us, or rather with me, for I forgot a parcel and he went back for it and Charlotte had to go on, as it was nearly dinner time, and she had to go home and see about it. He asked if some of us would walk round the point with him tomorrow and Miriam, Bella & I promised to go. We went to the Wainrights tonight to tea. Only ourselves. We were playing consequences, and Capt. Gore and I were together twice, Capt. Barry & I once, and Charlie Almon and I once Miriam, and Arthur Haliburton once, which I thought exquisite. We were dreadfully tired when we came home. Miriam had been up to Dutch Town with Charlotte Fairbanks in the morning.

March 3 Went to church and then down town with Charlotte. Parsons was the only man in church besides Uncle William. The paper this morning said that the *Halifax* only left Boston today. I cannot think what can have detained her so long. The only consolation is that by waiting so long in Boston, there is more chance of their getting the missing parcel. It was rather a dull day, but we went out with Cousin Ben and had a very pleasant walk indeed. The only thing was that I wore the boots I had on over on the Lakes and they were still so slippery that I could hardly walk in them and without Cousin Ben's help at times could not have got along at all. We came over the steep hill by the Martello Tower and found it one glare of ice. Cousin Ben slipped and could not stop himself until he was quite at the foot of the hill and I do not think he could stop then if there had not been some snow there to stop him. Miriam and Bella were venturesome enough to try the same but before they had gone two yards they both fell down and slid to the bottom. I crept along by the trees, swinging myself from one to the other, until Cousin Ben came back to help

Martello Tower, Point Pleasant Park, ca. 1870
The tower is one of two hundred towers built throughout the British
Empire during the eighteenth and early nineteenth centuries. Three were
built in Halifax as part of the British defenses. This particular tower
was erected between 1796 and 1798 to work in conjunction with the
fortifications of York Redoubt, the Citadel, George's Island, and
Sherbrooke Tower, and was manned from 1802 to 1875. This view
shows the tower prior to the removal of the roof, looking much as it did
during Sarah's visit.

me down quicker. We also missed a stone which we trusted, and slid some distance down the hill at a fearful rate, but being two together, held each other up, and did not fall though I was frightened enough. Mrs. Wilkins was at our house when we came home and gave me a letter from Aunt Eliza, which I opened without looking at the direction, and found it was for mother. I am so very tired, but read a little Spanish with Heber tonight. I was too tired to read any Latin. I bought a very pretty cedar wood box to put my drawing pencils in.

Mar. 4   Bella went out sleighing with Charlie Almon so I had to go down town alone, as she had intended to go with me. I met Cousin Ben on the way and he asked me to go round the point but the Hallegonians [sic] are so dreadfully proper that glad as I w'd have been, I did not quite like to. Aunt Mary said I might have gone for once. I met Capt. Barry and Arthur Haliburton on foot and I don't know how many riding. Perhaps it was as well I did not go with Cousin Ben, as I was very tired when

I reached home. There is a brigantine signaled, I hope it is the *Halifax*. Charlie Almon came up this evening and stayed until eleven o'clock. The papers say that Dr. Gray, Cousin Ben's grandfather, is dead at eight-six.[26]

March 5 ❧ First Sunday in Lent. Snow. The *Halifax* is signaled as having gone ashore, driven probably by the ice. A steamboat has gone down to help her off. I hope she will be up safe tomorrow. Uncle William preached this morning. Mr. Martin this afternoon. Heber read. The ice was so bad that Heber could not get to Falkland.

March 6 ❧ Morton's birthday. The steamer could not get the *Halifax* of[f] yesterday, and went down and tried today, but with no better success. The *Cumberland* is expected in today. It is an immense vessel. I took my first drawing lesson today. Miss McKie thinks I shall learn very well. She says I have a very good touch. It was so pleasant that when I came home, I persuaded Miriam to go out again with me coming back, we saw Capt. Barry riding with his funny Russian [sleigh] turn out just opposite Mrs. Wilkins's. He stopped and asked us if we would not ride. If we did one of us w'd have to drive as he would have to get out entirely. It is such a tiny sleigh. We refused, but he seemed so earnest to have us that at last we did and I drove, Capt. B. sitting in front at our feet. We drove around for about half an hour, enjoying it exceedingly, and when we came home, he asked us if we would go again tomorrow and we said yes, so he is to come for us tomorrow at three o'clock. He is such a perfect gentleman and so original, that it is a real pleasure to converse with him. I wrote an account of it home and a birthday note to Morton.

March 7 ❧ Capt. Barry came, time to the minute, and Miry and I jumped in and drove off. As soon as we reached the foot of Blisses hill, he gave me the reins, and sat as before, at our feet. We drove a long time, and met almost every one, and they all looked so astonished, for we are the first and only ladies Capt. Barry has ever taken out in Halifax. We went round the point and through Hollis, Granville and Barrington Streets, according to rule, and to say the least, ours was the most remarkable turnout in the town. We did enjoy it so much. Capt. Barry is so amusing and so intelligent and so odd, that he never wearies one. The *Halifax* was extricated and the Admiral's ship, the *Cumberland*, came in today. We spent the evening at Mrs. Binney's and Heber brought me my letters there. Such a number & a whole lot of newspapers.

March 8 ✐ Finished my letters home and went to church this morning, and then down to take my drawing lesson. Miriam went with me and came back as far as Mrs. Jonathan Allison's. Met Cousin Ben, who had asked Mr. Chainley to get us some seals, which he had done, and gave to us. I am in hopes Cousin Ben will take drawing lessons too. Have been writing all the afternoon and evening. It was very wet today, all the snow melting. Mr. Balfour told Bella as we were coming out of church that he had finished Wordsworth's "Apocalypse" that Heber lent him, and would return it today. I am glad for I want to finish it. He sent it down with a note saying that he had read it with intense interest and seemed very much pleased with it indeed. I did not go to church tonight. I intended to and actually had my things on, but I have a bad cold and it is very wet under foot and I changed my mind.

Mar. 9 ✐ I could not get the drawing book. I wanted to practice at home yesterday, so I went down for it today. It was so muddy. Bella was with me. Mr. Warren joined us and said he & Mr. Martin, Capt. Barry & some one else I did not know, had received their promotions, and he and Lieut. Martin had also received orders to return to England next Monday in the flag ship. They expect to be sent to Turkey when they get home, and appear greatly delighted. Capt. Barry will be dreadfully disappointed. He was talking so hopefully of receiving his orders day before yesterday. I am very glad he is promoted. We spent the evening at the Silvers. It was very pleasant, only the Misses Stairs besides ourselves. We came home quite early and found Mr. Balfour here. He always comes when I am not at home. I do not know how he always manages to hit the evenings so exactly. I suppose it is because I want to see him. I began a picture, a very small one, this afternoon.

Mar. 10 ✐ Finished my picture in a rather scratchy manner I fear, and wrote a letter to Uncle Morton, which I took down town and posted and stopped at Miss McKie on my way to get another pattern. Warren was there. He draws beautifully and is taking lessons in crayons and watercolours now. I suppose he

"Portrait of a woman,"
1840–1846, Mary McKie

Mary McKie was an amateur artist who lived in
Halifax. Her works were collected by Lady Falkland,
wife of the lieutenant-governor of Nova Scotia.
McKie remained amateur all her life, offering drawing
and painting lessons, which Sarah and several of her
friends attended.

"Nova Scotian Negro youth,"
Mary R. McKie, ca. 1840–1846

wants to do all he can, he is going away so soon. I am disappointed for he was going to take his lesson the hour that I do and perhaps Emily Wainwright & Dr. Grigor too and it would have been so very pleasant. I saw some very clever little etchings he did. Louisa, Miry and I were at Mrs. Thomson's this evening.

March 11   I worked about half my cloak collar today and feel as if I had been wonderfully industrious. Mr. Martin left his P.R.C. afternoon. We are invited to the Campbell's, Tuesday.

March 12   Heber read & Uncle W. preached this morning. This afternoon Uncle W. read & the Archdeacon preached. Heber brought an impression of the Seal of the Military Prison to me, from the Citadel. He went to Falkland today. Bella is laid up with a lame foot. The *Belle* has been due for nearly a week. I cannot think what has become of her.

March 13   The *Belle* is in. Have received two letters one from Mad. Doudiet, one from Mrs. Ward. I shall have the rest tomorrow. Took my third drawing lesson today.

March 14   Rest of my letters. Miss Morrisey made Tory's dress today. The flag ship H.M.S. *Cumberland* went out today. She looked perfectly majestic. Lieut. Warren and Martin went in her. We went to Mrs. Campbell's tonight in Mr. Murdock's carriage. I was very tired and did not want to go, neither did Tory, but we were obliged to.

March 15   Received a letter from Uncle Morton enclosing five pounds. Went to Dutch town this afternoon to see Mrs. McCulla with Charlotte but did not stay long as I was fearful of tiring her. We called also at Mrs. Gardiner's, Misses Black, Mme Duport and Mrs. Mukrel. Miss Black returned me a handkerchief I left there the night of the party there. Wrote home. Went to church morning and evening. Took a drawing lesson.

March 16   Wrote to Uncle Morton and Aunt Eliza. Enclosed Aunt Eliza's note to Cousin Ben asking him at the same time to come up this evening, which he accordingly did and was very pleasant. [He] appeared to take a great interest in my seals, and says he will see if he has one to give me.

March 17 ⌇ St. Patrick's day. Went to St. George's to morning church, and stayed to try the organ at Mr. Uniacke's advice. He appeared quite pleased, and stayed there with me more than an hour. I came up to Dutch town again in the afternoon to call. Heber and Charlotte came with me. When we came home I found a little parcel from Cousin Ben containing a number of seals and cards, and a little note. Some of the seals are very pretty. Mrs. Uniacke has invited Heber, Louisa and me to dine with her next Monday and Mr. U. will take us out to drive in the afternoon to Princes' Lodge.

March 18 ⌇ Drew a picture at home (not very well) and wrote home.

March 19 ⌇ Sacrament Sunday, 3rd Sunday in Lent. The Bishop preached in the morning and read prayers in the afternoon. Heber preached in the afternoon. The Bishop preached upon the Cleansing of the Leper and Heber upon the text "To run ye that may obtain." Both were most excellent, eloquent, practical sermons. I like the Bishop better each time I hear him. He reads remarkably well. Strangely enough the second lesson this afternoon was the duty of a Bishop. He flushed a good deal, but read it very steadily and well.

March 20 ⌇ Drew. I am going to take four lessons a week instead of two in order to do as much as I can before I go home. Dr. Grigor takes lessons in oil Mondays & Wednesday. He thinks I have a great talent for drawing. Mrs. Uniacke sent me a note to say that Mr. Uniacke had an engagement and could not take us for a ride, so we only went to dinner. Mr. & Mrs. Wilkins, Tory & Miriam and Dr. Munro were the only guests besides ourselves. We had a very pleasant evening and came home in Mrs. W.'s carriage.

March 21 ⌇ Drew. The Misses Blacks draw Tuesdays & Fridays so I have a very pleasant class both times. Tomorrow is my birthday. I hope the *Halifax* will be in, tho I hardly expect it. It w'd be such a nice birthday present. Today Mrs. Wilkins wants me to teach her Spanish, so I went and gave her a first lesson today. Went down town with Charlotte to ask Cousin Ben to come up tomorrow, as it is my birthday.

"Man and woman sleighing,"
William Smyth Maynard Wolfe, 1853–1854

Sleighing, especially in Point Pleasant Park,
was a popular social activity for middle-
and upper-class Haligonians.

March 22 🙠 Such a happy birthday, a beautiful day. I went down to take my drawing lesson and began a picture that I am going to send to Uncle Morton on his birthday. I thought it would be nice to begin it, my birthday for his. It is a view of Donegall Abbey, Ireland. Very pretty but rather hard. My presents were a most beautiful rosewood workbox, lined with green satin & silver paper, finished with mother of pearl and silver, from the whole family. Kebly's Christian year from Heber, and Coopers works from Cousin Ben, a collar from Mrs. Wilkins. Dr. Grigor gave me a painting of our coat of arms yesterday, which I can call a birthday present and a number of cards. Cousin Ben came up this evening and stayed quite late. Wrote a note to mother and father. The *Halifax* did not come in. Cousin Ben is pleasant. Charlotte & Bella went to hear Dr. Grigor's lecture on Adyle?

March 23 🙠 I was downtown today and when I came home I was most agreeably surprised to find a parcel from home awaiting me. A birthday parcel and a good sized one too. It was in Halifax yesterday, but the man did not know where to bring it. A letter from Mother, a partial letter from father, one from Mary Pope, with a silk dress from home, and a most beautiful Prayer Book to match my Bible were my presents. We spent the evenings at Mrs. Twinings (Mrs. Charles). Cassie is going to the states next steamer. In the parcel from home was a daguerreotype of Molly & Beppo. Went to see Mrs. McCulla and took her a bouquet.

March 24 🙠 Took another drawing lesson. Finished sketching the piece I began last Wednesday for Uncle Morton. I think it is very pretty. It is a view of Donegall Abby, Ireland. I am going to shade it with lithographic chalks. It is on tinted paper, the lights to be put in with Chinese white. We went to Mrs. Grove's this evening and I began a collar, I do not know if I shall ever finish it. Dr. Grigor gave me a number of cards. Went to church this morning.

March 25 🙠 Went this evening to Mrs. Wilkin's. Very pleasant, but very noisy. I took refuge from the noise in chess with Mr. Binney, but he beat me both times. Cousin Ben and he walked home with us, and he gave me a box of seals he had promised Heber to get for us. We heard that Mr. Balfour was thrown from his horse the other day, or rather with his horse, for his horse fell, catching his fore feet in a deep rut or hole in the road. Mr. Balfour is always managing to tumble down some how or other. Fortunately he was not much hurt but his regimentals were.

March 26 — Fourth Sunday in Lent. The wind is exceedingly high with a little snow in the air. More drifting than falling I fancy. I did not go to church this evening. I seldom do for Sunday evening the gas is so powerful and the church is dreadfully crowded.

March 27 — My ninth drawing lesson. I regret more and more every day that I did not begin when I first came. Miss McKie says I might have been in water colours now if I had. We went to the association with Cousin Ben this evening and were much amused but dreadfully tired and almost deafened by the ranting and shouting of Mr. Jones, the lecturer.

March 28 — Miss Morrisey came to make my Argentine. She has made it very well indeed. I took a short drawing lesson, as I was obliged to go downtown to get some things for her. I met a great many people. R. Haliburton walked down as far as Dr. Moyer's with me, met among others, A. Haliburton, N. Zwicker, Cousin Ben, Col. Murray, Mr. Walker and Mr. Bland (engineer). Did not go to Mr. Wilkin's.

March 29 — Louisa's birthday. She had a workbox as much like mine as she could get it. Heber gave her Longfellow's Golden Legend & Mr. Jones gave her a most beautiful diamond ring. I went to church morning and evening and took a good drawing lesson. I get on much faster now that I take four lessons a week. I have got in all the background of my piece and begun the ruin itself.

March 30 — Went downtown with Charlotte. In the evening Cousin Ben came up and played chess till quite late. Tory & I played against Bella and him and beat them at last, after some fluctuations of fortune.

March 31 — At breakfast this morning we heard that the *Belle* was rundown by the *Hesnic* on its way to Halifax. While we were speaking about it, a letter came to me by mail, saying that mother had not written by the *Belle* on account of her being at Manchester when the *Belle* sailed and she wrote by the steamer for fear I should be anxious at not receiving any letters by her. Capt. Meagher (of the *Belle*) escaped almost by a miracle for he was struck senseless by the falling of a block and only recovered when he was six inches under water on the deck of the *Belle*, which sunk three minutes after being struck. He caught at a rope, which fortunately was within his reach, and was taken up, but two people were lost in her. I took a short drawing lesson and went to church and to Mrs. Wilkins's, where I found a letter from Aunt Eliza for me. Miriam, Louisa and I went out calling in the afternoon and made eleven calls. Spent the evening at Mrs. McCulla's. Mr. Boggs walked home with us.

April 1   One of the worst storms of wind and rain that there has ever been since I have been here. Miss Morrisey came to make Charlotte's dress. The water pipe burst and flooded the kitchen, but Uncle W. succeeded in stopping it after a while.

April 2   A most beautiful day after one of the stormiest nights that ever kept me awake. The air is so mild and balmy that the boys got chairs out on the verandah. Uncle William had the whole service this morning, and Mr. Maturin this afternoon. Heber was at St. Paul's. Uncle W. is sick this evening. Cousin Ben walked home from church with us.

April 3   Charlotte went with me to draw today. I finished the piece I was doing and better than I expected to. Miss McKie mounted it for me. I have only taken thirteen lessons and she says I have done very well. Bella called for me to go shopping and coming back we met Cousin Ben who took us to see the closing of the House. We went round the point afterwards to get some seaweeds for Miriam but did not succeed very well. Met a good many people; among others, Mr. Balfour, twice; the Bishop; several of the Almons, among others Ella & Annie, who walked up with us; The Seward, Mr. Bland (72nd), Ward, Tutersue, Beamish. Capt Dirk & Miriam went to Mr. Uniacke's this evening and came back when she had gone. A little was to call our attention to a comet in the west very near where the one was last summer. It does not appear as large (or as near) as that one was. The Flag Ship (*Vestal*) came in today.

April 4   I brought home my drawing today, finished and mounted. They said it was very well done. I went downtown with Louisa to shop and so missed Cousin Ben who called for me to go round the point with him. Tory and Bella went instead. He left a chess problem for me to find out. I met the Archdeacon who told me that he had just parted from Sir Gaspard who said that Uncle Morton was appointed Bail Bond Commissioner. I got a pair of gloves and a book for Molly's birthday present. Cousin Ben met me coming home and walked up with me. Charlie Gore came up in the evening to teach his algebra lesson. Heber asked me to work out a sum for him but I could not.

April 5 Went down to my drawing lesson. Did not do much today, as it was muddy and I had to hold up my new dress. But consequently my hand shook so that I could hardly hold the pencil. I brought home my book to set my drawings, but I left it by mistake at Mrs. Wilkins's where I stopped to give Sadie a Spanish lesson. Went to church morning & evening. A man was baptized this morning. Bella and I were coming up Hollis St. and were joined by Charlie Almon, who of course devoted himself to Bella, leaving me alone to be victimized by Tuck Grigor, who also joined us. I was so provoked. I was too tired to talk to please him, so he had the most of it to do himself. I got some ribbon down town to make Beppo an English flag for his birthday present.

April 6 Beppo is a year old today. We all wished many happy returns to his daguerreotype. I got my drawing book, or rather Heber did for me, as it rained and I did not go out. I did my drawings this evening. I also began Beppo's flag, and did as much as I could of it, but found that I had not quite ribbon enough. We had dates after dinner, for dessert in honor of Beppo. It seems a great while since I had letters.

April 7 I finished Beppo's flag and am going to get some of the large wooden knitting needles for a flag staff. The Confirmation was held at St. Paul's this morning. I went there from drawing. The service was a most impressive one. I think the Bishop is particularly excellent in the Sacraments and Rites of the church. His prayer and address at the close were most earnest and eloquent. Mr. Wilkins went to Windsor this morning. Heber, applying for the curacy of St. Paul's [which is] about to become vacant, finds himself unexpectedly opposed by Mr. G. Hill, but he is sure of success, as Uncle William is promised two thirds of the votes at the very least.

April 8 🍃 I began to finish the antimacassar for Aunt Mary's birthday this morning. I went downtown immediately after breakfast to match the thread in which I succeeded better than I expected and to get the flag staff for Beppo. I have taken cold and did not go out again all day. Dr. & Mrs. Donald, Mrs. Johnston and Miss Wentworth, and Miss Stevens called. Heber resigned the curacy of St. Paul's. I bound two collars this evening.

April 9 🍃 Rather a dull day. I have quite a cold. Uncle William preached this morning and the Archdeacon this afternoon. Uncle W. this evening. The *Halifax* came in very late last night and I cannot get my letter and parcel until tomorrow evening. It is rather tantalizing to have them here two days and not able to get them. I shall go to drawing at nine tomorrow so as to get two hours before church. After this week the lessons will not be so broken up as they have been during Lent.

April 10 🍃 Drew. Begun a new piece, a ruin. Came to church at eleven. It rained very heavily but we went to church in the evening to hear Heber. His topic was the saints. I fancy Mr. Dunn's tomorrow will be rather different. Heber did not deliver it as well as usual. The light was so bad that he could hardly see. This morning Mr. Balfour came home from church with Uncle William to see Shepherds opinion of receiving the Holy Communion on Good Friday. It is to be administered at St. Paul's but not at St. Luke's and he did not quite know which to do. Shepherd thinks that as it is a feast prepared by Christ to be received with joy and thankfulness, we are hardly in an appropriate state to receive it on Good Friday, the most mournful feast of the year. That it is not absolutely wrong, but not in strict accordance with the discipline of the church. Mr. Balfour staid nearly two hours. I showed him the flag I was making for Beppo, which I had finished. Heber brought me my letters after afternoon school. There were special crochet and embroidery patterns from Mrs. Barker for us.

April 11 🍃 Drew and went to church. Afterwards went downtown with Bella to get a pair of rubbers. We had to get sandals as there were no good rubber shoes in town. We met a great many people. Mr. Parsons came up in the afternoon to bid us good-bye. He is under orders to return to England on the next steamer and is in perfect ecstasies about it. He hopes to have Sir

George Seymour as fellow passenger.[27] I finished my letters home as the *Halifax* will probably sail tomorrow or next day. I copied Mr. Jones' register of the thermometer for Mr. Bond. We went to church in the evening. Mr. Dunn preached, sat in Col. Fergus' pew.

April 12   The *Bermuda Mail* was signaled very early this morning. Dr. Munro, as was expected, returned in her. I went down to draw and returned to church. After church Uncle W. had a class for those who had been confirmed and were to receive the Communion next Sunday. I also attended and afterwards wrote a note to Uncle Morton and took it down town to post it. Returning I met Heber and Mr. Balfour walking. Heber was taking my letters down to Capt. O'Brien, making poor Mr. Balfour go too, who I suppose wished I were not quite so epistolary a young lady. Bella and I afterwards walked down the point, we met Heber and Mr. Balfour again, and met many people. Cousin Ben met us and we walked together. We did not get home until nearly six o'clock. We went to church again in the evening. Uncle William preached. Heber says that Capt. Meagher and his men are going to board the *Arabia* tonight when she comes in, to demand restitution or at least compensation of the loss of the *Belle*. I suppose it is a sort of form. Went to church this evening. Mr. Maturin preached upon the Paschal Lamb. Mr. Dunn's sermon night before last was upon the Offering up of Isaac. I was quite astonished at his sermon. I had no idea that he could write such a good one. It was not more to be compared to Heber's the night before than the gas (which is now very bad) to the sun. But still it was more I am sure than anyone could have expected from him. Uncle William's last night was upon the Brazen Serpent. The Bishop himself will preach tomorrow upon the type of the Scape Goat. Mr. Wilkin's said the other day that he thinks Uncle Morton will be down in a day or two upon meeting of the Railway Commissioners.[28] I hope it is true and that he will come down. I was so tired when I came home, and so was Bella, that we both bade good-night, but before we had either of us begun to undress, a ring came to the door and said that it was Dr. Munro. We hastily rushed our hair, put on cuffs and descended in due form. We were laughed at a little. Dr. Munro is much handsomer than I expected, but looks very much as I thought he would. He is very gentlemanly and agreeable, but looked tired and walked dizzily as I soon well remembered is usually the case, with those coming from a vessel of any description. I think I shall like him very much.

April 13   I was too tired to get up as early as usual, but was able to work a little before breakfast. Went to church, and when I came home, crocheted a little, but got on rather slowly. Mr. Uniacke & Chipman called to say that he was going to Boston in the steamer expected tonight and to ask for a letter of introduction to father, which I gave him. He is to stay about six weeks.

April 14   Good Friday. Went to church three times. In the evening Miriam and I went down very early as I wished to go and look at the organ. The bishop's sermon was exceedingly beautiful showing much learning made of practical use. Much earnestness, making by every sympathy, everyone else in earnest too, much clearness of judgment and power of explaining himself clearly which is not very common, and much fearlessness in battling with daring popular errors and favorite faults. But I think even he must yield the palms to Heber whose sermon has been the best of the week so far and I do not think Mr. Gilpin will excel him tomorrow.

April 15   Went to church morning and evening, and worked on Aunt Mary's antimacassar in the afternoon. Mr. Gilpin preached a very good sermon indeed upon the life of the prophet Jonah. The bishop walked part of the way home with us. Yesterday the new Admirals have come to relieve Sir George Seymour. There was a great deal of saluting going on and Sir George went home in the return steamer. Capt. Meagher detained the Arabia some hours, as he intended.

April 16   Easter Sunday. Uncle William preached this morning and Heber read. There were one hundred and sixteen communicants. At St. Paul's there were one hundred and fifty-seven. I do not know how many of the Military were at the Garrison Chapel. Tory and Bella remained for the first time. I was too tired to go to church this evening. Dr. Munro walked up from church this morning with Mr. Jones. He did not stay very long. He says he is coming up tomorrow or Tuesday to tea. He does not like the small bonnets now the fashion. He is in hopes of being sent to Turkey.

April 17   Went to my drawing lesson. Came back to church. Went down to Mrs. Wilkin's but Sadie was not at home, so I went down town with Louisa. I forgot to say yesterday that Lady Le Marchant's little boy was christened in the afternoon by the bishop at St. Paul's. His name was Seymour [indecipherable] Halifax. His sponsors Sir George and Lady Seymour by their proxies. Mr. Bosworth and Mrs. Norman Uniacke and the Archdeacon stood proxy for someone else. It snowed this evening so that Dr. Munro did not come up. I finished Aunt Mary's antimacassar.

April 18   It rained but I went down to draw. It cleared up just in time for Miss Grigor's wedding. Louisa went down with Mr. Kinnear and said it was a very nice wedding. Heber brought me the news that Uncle Morton was in town so I wrote him a little note asking him to come to tea but did not come until after nine. He was very pleasant and agreeable and I was so glad to find that I remembered him. He looked exactly as I remembered him, only a little bald. He has such a sweet smile. I am so very glad to have seen him, tho it was rather [indecipherable] to hear him say as he bade me good bye, that he is going to Windsor tomorrow morning. So after all I have seen him but a couple of hours, but that was a pleasure that I would not have lost for a very great deal. I am so glad to have seen him.

April 19   Went down to draw. Charlotte went to try to catch a glimpse of Uncle M. but I suppose I was too late. I hope he will be down again soon. Went to church this evening and met Heber and walked a little way afterwards. Bought a sketchbook as Miss McKie wants me to try to sketch.

April 20   Aunt Mary's birthday. The girls gave her a handsome habit shirt and sleeves and such a pretty little cap and a bottle of lavender, her favorite perfume. I gave her the antimacassar which Ellen had done up beautifully for me. She is very obliging indeed. After breakfast I helped Louisa all day to make blanc mange, lemon creams &c. for a few friends who are coming this evening in honor of Aunt Mary's birthday. I must stop for it is almost time for them to arrive.

All our party came. Not one disappointment but Mrs. Lyttleton, who had a friend staying with her and could not come. Beside ourselves, there was Bessie & Rebecca Rand, Dora Bell, Mary & Louisa Bliss & Lewis, Mr. Jones, Mrs. Bland, Mr. Balfour, Dr. Munro, Mr. C. Allison. Just before it broke up Mr. Jones was talking to Dr. Munro and fainted. Dr. Munro said he should not have attempted to come up tonight. We did not expect it at all. Dr. M. seems to think him very ill indeed. He thinks the aneurism has made great progress. With that exception, the evening was a remarkably pleasant one. Rebecca Rand plays remarkably well and Dora Bell sings with much taste, but without much power. I wore my green dress for the 1st time.

April 21 Mr. Jones was quite well this morning and went to school both morning and afternoon. I went down to draw. Miriam and I were alone in the house in the afternoon and Capt. Thompson of H.M.S. *Vestal* called. We had a very pleasant time and he stayed a long time and made himself very agreeable. He is very gentlemanly. We were invited to Mrs. McCulla's this evening but were engaged to Mrs. Moren's. Miriam & I went. She wore her white and I my green. I was too tired to enjoy it much but appeared a very pleasant party. Dr. Munro came up today at one o'clock and went all over the house as he has had no opportunity before. He is very nice indeed. So agreeable and gentlemanly and also says everything in a different way from any one else. He made Bella promise to wear her hair banded plain round her face which is much more becoming than the old way.

April 22 I am very tired after Mrs. Moren's party yesterday. Heber and Mr. Balfour went out to the Three Mile House and Heber brought back some very pretty mayflowers. Miriam spent the evening at Miss Grove's. The boys took their dinner out to the woods and did not come home till quite late. Aunt Mary began to grow quite anxious about them before they made their appearance. This afternoon Uncle William was out in the garden and Miriam and I were the only ones in the house for Mr. Jones who was at home in the first part of the afternoon. Went out to return a book to Mr. Balfour and Capt. Thomson of H.M.S. *Vestal* called. Uncle W. came in from the garden and Capt. Thomson made a very long and agreeable call. He is very gentlemanly, though by no means a handsome or very elegant looking man. The Archdeacon called but left a message at the door as Uncle W. had gone out after Capt. Thomson left and was on horseback. I am dreadfully tired and glad enough not to have to go out tonight as Mary had to.

April 23 We were aroused very early this morning by the alarming intelligence that Mr. Sawyer's house was on fire, but afterwards discovered that it was across the street, but still, Mr. Sawyer was in danger of having his house injured. Four small houses and five stables were burned. Mr. Maturin preached this afternoon and Uncle W. this morning. Heber went to Falkland. Dr. Munro came up for a few minutes between churches. It is St. George's day, but being Sunday will be celebrated tomorrow when the bishop will deliver a sermon.

April 24 ❦ Molly's birthday. Mr. Jones was kept awake all night with his cough and this morning at breakfast fainted from exhaustion, but laid down for about an hour and then got up and said he felt very much better but thought it better not to go out. We went to church and heard a most splendid sermon. Early in the morning I took some roses down to Cousin Ben that I had promised him. Coming back from church Mary and I were together and met Mr. Charman who invited us to go and see the procession from his house and afterwards to stay to lunch and go out driving with them in the afternoon. We had a very nice lunch and a very pleasant drive round the point and then through the town and beyond the Admiralty, towards Three Mile House. We, that is Tory, Bella and I, are to spend the evening at Capt. Lyttleton's.

April 25 ❦ Mr. Jones is dead.[29] He died at seven o'clock this afternoon. We went to Mrs. Lyttleton's last night, but was very tired driving so long, and did not enjoy it much, particularly as Mr. Tuck Grigor, whom I do not like at all, trapped me into a game of chess, a most stupid thing to do at a party. I danced but three times. First with Charlie Almon, next with Mr. Aughton of H.M.S. *Vestal*, and next with T. Grigor. I sat by Tory a greater part of the evening looking at pictures. From not spending a very pleasant evening it was less of a shock than might have been expected, though bad enough at best, to be hushed on coming into our own home by the intelligence that Mr. Jones was insensible and might not live through the night. Dr. Munro had just left him and his heavy breathing caused by the anuerism resounded through the hushed house with frightful regularity and distinctness. Heber looked more distressed than I have ever seen him. Neither he nor Uncle William or Aunt Mary, Charlotte or Louisa would go to bed but insisted on our going. It was nearly four o'clock when I went to bed and about seven when we got up. We were surprised to find that Mr. Jones was still alive but still insensible, in such state he remained till his death. Last night when we went out he was drinking tea and looking better than he had all day. Aunt Mary says that at nine o'clock, when he went to bed, he dropped his medicine himself and went up stairs for his watch key and wound up his watch. Not ten minutes after Dr. Munro came in and went to his room where he found him lying on the bed almost insensible. He just managed to undress him and got him into bed when total insensibility came on accompanied by this heavy breathing. This morning Mr. Balfour's orderly brought Heber two Spanish books & was given a message to Mr. B. to say that Mr. J. was dying. Before we thought the orderly could have reached in the barracks, Mr. B. was down. He came four times during the day and was going to sit up with him, if he had lived. The Blisses have put down their curtains out of sympathy & delicacy to Aunt M and Uncle W. as soon as they saw ours closed. Dr. Munro has been down several times, once just now quite late. Aunt Mary and Louisa are quite worn out. Louisa slept some time on the sofa today. The bishop sent Mr. Maturin up twice to inquire after Mr. J., once just as he died. A trunk came from home about a quarter of an hour before he died, to me.

April 26   A letter came from Mr. Jones's mother a few hours before he died yesterday. My trunk brought me a pretty morning dress, Josey's likeness, letters, scrapbook, boots and several other things. The boots are too large so Charlotte is going to take them and I will send for a smaller pair. The *Halifax* came in today bringing me a very very pretty pink opera sack from mother, of her own working, for a birthday present to me. I have been all day writing funeral notes for Uncle William, inviting the personal friends of Mr. Jones to his funeral, day after tomorrow. There is a very large fire apparently in Barracks this evening.

April 27   A colored man named Henry Jordan, who lives in Digby, came to Halifax yesterday and has come up to help Uncle William in anything he could do for him. He cleaned all the [silver] plate in the house today most beautifully. Drs. Almon, Bell & Parker, had an examination or autopsy of Mr. Jones today. Dr. Munro would take no part in it, merely stayed in the room. If he had lived till Friday, he would have died of hemorrhage.

April 28   Mr. Jones was buried today. A very large number of persons, besides those invited, attended. The clergy all attended in their gowns and the whole school attended in a body, also several of their former scholars. I wrote home today, as the *Halifax* goes out tomorrow. I forgot to say that the bonnet block came in the trunk. I do not know whether we shall like the shape or not. It is a rather peculiar one.

April 29 I wrote to Uncle Morton today so that the stage may take up the parcel on Monday. Dr. Munro came in this evening as I was writing a letter and insisted upon seeing my hand-writing. I did not want him to see that leaf, for it was particularly badly written, but he mistook the cause of my hesitation and said rather reproachfully that he would not read a word. As if it entered my head to suspect he would. Rather that he should think that I told him plainly the reason I had refused. Tory had caught the leaf and given it to him. He said, "Well, the writing was very legible" he could not say good. I sealed some letters for Heber and sewed a little.

April 30 Aunt Mary is quite ill today. Dr. Munro came up between churches to see her and commented upon the size, or rather want of size, of my bonnet. Mr. Parminter preached this afternoon, but I don't think any one heard a word he said. I could not and I heard a great many others, who sat very near, make the same complaint. One or two who did hear, said that we had lost nothing. Dr. Munro came in again tonight and stayed some time. I copied part of the thermometer register for Mr. Bond.

May 1 Rained. Aunt Mary is much better. I went down to draw, and Miss McKie lent me a paper on perspective which I have copied. Mr. Jones's books and trunks came over from Miss Lovett's today, for he left all his books to Heber and all the rest of his property, except 'Me Eing', to Louisa. There are some most valuable works in his library. Dr. Munro came in this after-noon to see Aunt M. and made me a very nice pen indeed. So nice that Louisa and Mary asked him to make them each one, which he did.

May 2 Uncle Morton's birthday. I went down to draw and finished and brought home 'Abbotsford', a piece I have just finished. Uncle W. thinks that I have improved very much. I am to begin Loch Awe tomorrow. Bella and I went down to the point and met Heber who gathered us some Mayflowers. The bish-op passed & spoke to us & T. Grigor stopped and talked until Heber came back, when we gave him a polite dismissal most gladly.

May 3   Went down to draw. Sketched in Lock Awe and then went down town to church with Aunt M. and Louisa, and afterwards went shopping. I tried to get a bonnet, but could not please myself, so will wait for some which are coming in the steamer soon. I got a black lace veil, which I wanted very much, at Duffus & Tupper's. Met Mrs. Robie downtown who asked me if I would take a message for her the next time I wrote home, about her servant Dawber. I spent the afternoon arranging Mr. Jones's books in Heber's room. Uncle W. put up the shelves this morning. I was so flushed and tired with lifting the heavy books when Dawber came that I was quite mystified when I went down to find that Adelaide had shown him into the parlor and Mr. Balfour had come in with Heber and was there too. So I took the message as quick as I could and got him away. Mr. B. brought such a funny looking dog with him named Squib, with long, grey silky hair; a Skye Terrier. Mary and I went down to spend the evening at Mr. Stewart, Master of the Rolls. On our way we met Lewis Bliss, who gave me a lovely bunch of may flowers, which I took down with me. They have a very pretty house inside, though it is very ugly and old looking outside. We had a very pleasant evening.

May 5   Drew. Began to read "Widow Barneby" and think it very amusing. Bought a frame to cover with leather works for Uncle Morton. I only got one box of labels for the books and put them all on, but find it not enough. Heber is going to get another box tomorrow. We are house cleaning. The sweeps have been here today.

May 6   Finished labeling and numbering and marking a catalogue of the books. Dr. Munro came in today and seemed quite surprised to find Charlotte's room converted for the time, into a parlor and a very pretty one too. This evening it has been both snowing and hailing.

May 7   Snow and frost. It is quite cold today. Heber preached this morning and Mr. Maturin this afternoon. Heber went to Dartmouth this evening Louisa with him. Charlie Lloyd came in after church and stayed to tea. He is a handsome boy with immense dark blue eyes. I finished my home letters tonight, as the *Kingston* goes tomorrow probably. I met such a pretty passage in the Confession of St. Augustine that I copied it for mother about when he was a baby. It begins [indecipherable].

May 8 🙠 Drew, but did not feel well and left the class before twelve. Wrote to Uncle Morton to ask him for some money and Miriam went down with me to post the letter and one she had written to R. Rand. Met Cousin Ben on the way and he walked with us a little while and then had to leave as Miry and I went down to the battery & then back. We were dreadfully tired. The Kingston, while I was watching it going down the harbor, a note came from Cousin Ben asking me to enclose a letter from him the next time I wrote. If I had known it a few hours before, I could have sent it today. The children went to Gen. Gore's this evening. It is Fred Gore's birthday and he gave a child's party. Charlotte is spending the day at Mrs. McCulla's.

General C. Gore, ca.1865
Gore was the Commander of British Forces and husband of Sarah Fraser, the daughter of James Fraser. While stationed at Halifax, the couple and their children resided at the elegant Bellevue House.

May 9 🙠 Went down to draw and finished the piece I was doing. 'Loch Awe.' Uncle William thinks I improved very fast. I do not feel very well and was glad to be able to decline an invitation to Miss Grove's this evening. I was out shopping all the afternoon with Aunt Mary, Louisa & Charlotte. I bought some ribbons to trim a bonnet and a bunch of lilies of the valley for my white crochet, which Charlotte stiffened for me this morning. There is a brigantine signaled. I hope it is the *Halifax*. Lewis Bliss spent the evening here. In the first part of the evening, before he came, I was in the parlor helping Tory with her French exercise and did not go into the room where he was till about ten o'clock. Louisa's room is used for the present as a parlor; as there is no coal in Halifax and we can only burn wood in an air tight stove, and there is one in that room.

May 10 ⌀   Drew today. I want to practice foliage and began a large elm tree but felt rather discouraged with the result. I can sketch it in very tolerably, but when I begin to shade, all appearance of a tree vanishes, not in to thin air, but into lead pencil dust. My head ached so that I had to stop about twelve. Coming away I met Mrs. Wilkins and as there was a pleasant breeze, I thought it would do my head good to walk on with her, so I went to see the new Market House and the Reading Room. Met Cousin Ben & Heber. Heber went with us, but cousin Ben only stayed with us a little while. He has a very bad cold. He wants us to go out for May flowers after a day or two. Miss Fraser was with Mrs. Wilkins. I did not know before that she was in town. So in the afternoon Miry & I went up to Dutch town to call upon her. Mrs. Uniacke wants two of us to go up & spend Friday with her. We met Cousin Ben on the way, and he went up with us. Mr. Uniacke gave us a number of books and slips for the garden in which Uncle William takes a very great interest. Among others, Mr. U gave us several suckers of a large elm tree which he planted twenty three years ago, on condition that we shall plant them ourselves, which we did, Cousin Ben, Miry & I when we came home. Went to church in the evening. Uncle W. preached. The steamer came in as we went to church.

May 11 ⌀   Began a dark crochet bonnet for the mornings instead of buying a straw, as I do not like the shapes out and very much like the block. Bought a brooch for Josey, but it is not so pretty as mine. I could not get one like it. Finished one breadth of my skirt. It is Lizzy Pope's birthday.

May 12 ⌀   Drew. Charlotte and I went up to Mrs. Uniacke's at two o'clock. I took my bonnet to work on, but did not do as much as I intended. Lady went on horseback with Mr. Uniacke. She looked very pretty. Andy & Fitz Uniacke came in to dinner and Heber came up in the evening and with Miss Fraser & Mrs. Wilkins & Sady & Miriam made quite a party. In the afternoon I went to the church to the choir practice. We had a most delightful walk home.

May 13 ⌀   Uncle W. said this morning that the *Halifax* came in yesterday while I was at Mrs. Uniacke's. I was so glad. And better than I expected; he brought me the letters at noon, one from

Bellevue House, ca. 1860

Bellevue House was located at the corner of Spring Garden Road and Queen Street and was the official residence of the officer commanding His Majesty's forces in Nova Scotia and/or British North America. During Sarah's stay it was the home to General and Mrs. Gore.

mother, one from Josey, one from Molly, & one from Mad. Doudiet. Cousin Ben sent up to know if some of us could like to go to Down's for May flowers & to see the birds. So Miry & I went at two o'clock. It was very warm, but pleasant, but unfortunately I had on a pair of stiff English boots and my feet are covered with blisters, but to make up for it, I have received my parcel from home. Heber went after it, tired as he was after rowing eight miles with Dr. Munro & Dr. Grigor against the tide & a dead calm. Mother sent me two very pretty dresses & gloves & several things I wanted. Among others, two pair of American boots. Mr. Balfour & Rev. M. Par__ called this afternoon, and they made very pleasant visits. Cousin Ben looked dreadfully tired and had to go to a party in the evening. Poor fellow. Mother has not yet written to say where they have moved.

May 14   Uncle W. preached this morning & the Archdeacon this afternoon. Uncle W. again this evening. Louisa lined and arranged the flowers in my white crochet bonnet yesterday and I was very glad to have it to wear today as it was very warm. I wore my green dress & shawl and felt comfortable for the first time for a month almost. My winter clothes are so oppressive. I wrote home and wrote in German to Mad. Doudiet.

May 15   Drew. Went out shopping with Charlotte. Brought some ribbon for my bonnet & crepe to line my crochet but one very nice thing I found by [chance], some gutta puncha cloth to put in my bonnets. My hair, generally wet before I go out, ruins my bonnet linings. Late this evening, and quite unexpected, the postman brought me a letter from Uncle Morton containing five pounds.

May 16   Drew. Finished crocheting my dark crochet bonnet and began a flower white one for Miry. Wrote to Uncle Morton to acknowledge his last letter, and sent two or three papers to Aunt Eliza.

May 17   The Fast day appointed by Government in account of the war. The Bishop preached they say, a very fine sermon this morning at St. Paul's and Uncle W. as I know, a very fine one at St. Luke's. But Heber's in the afternoon was one of the best I have every heard him preach. Mr. Maturin this evening was a miserable disappointment. I was so glad that the Bishop and all the clergy heard Heber. There was an excellent congregation in the afternoon. All the clergy of Halifax except those of St. George's parish were there. Only Uncle William was at Falkland. I forgot him. In the evening a man in church had a fit. He was sitting behind Mr. Balfour who started up and I believe assisted him. So Tory said, who sat nearer than I did. I rec'd a letter from Aunt Eliza saying that Uncle Storrs wanted to know when I was going to Cornwallis. So I wrote to both her and Uncle Storrs. There were about 710 pounds collected in St. Paul's parish for the relief of the wives and children of the soldiers who were ordered to Turkey. Mr. Spur of Mahone Bay came up after morning church.

May 18 ⤳ Posted my letter to Aunt E. and Uncle Storrs. Worked on the white crochet bonnet, but not a great deal. Wore for the first time the little pink negligee that mother sent me with my green silk. It looks very pretty. Charlotte and Bella went to a concert tonight with Charlie Almon. The concert is given by a Mr. Outram. I helped Louisa a very little to arrange the drawing rooms in their blue summer dress in lieu of their red winter robes.

May 19 ⤳ Drew. I am now drawing a shore piece by Harding with a good many puffins in it. Went out shopping with Louisa on the strength of the five pounds Uncle Morton sent me. I bought a beige dress and Louisa bought a muslin mantle, very pretty. I also bought the paper &c. to fit up Charlotte's desk & the linings of the dresses Miss Morrisey is to make for me. I expect her tomorrow. We met Dr. Munro. It was the first time he had seen me in a summer dress and he did not recognize me immediately. He promised to come up and spend the evening but has not come. It is a very long time since he has been up. Mr. Rowley came up form Yarmouth today & brought a letter from Mary. I put a tuck in my chintz morning dress today as it was too long. All that I did today is the crochet bonnet. I had to take it out, as it is too small for the present style, and I must enlarge it. Uncle W. had a communion class today. It was not very fully attended.

May 20 ⤳ I am disappointed as Miss Morrisey did not come today after I had made all the preparations for her. If she comes next week I shall have to give up one of my drawing lessons if not more. As I have four dresses, at least, to be made before I go to Windsor. I am afraid I shall be hurried at the last. Louisa has been looking over all her goods to see what she will want for her

"Point Pleasant Battery,"
by Alexander Cavalié Mercer, 1842

Remnants of this battery and other fortifica-
tions are still visible throughout the park,
which was constructed to protect the harbour.

visit. I hope she will be at Cornwallis too. Mr. Rowley called again in the afternoon and Heber brought in some superb May flowers. Mr. Rowley says that soap & water keeps the flowers better than plain water. Charlotte and Louisa went to Miss Grove's tonight.

May 21 Communion Sunday. The number of Communicants was not so large as usual. Uncle William preached this morning and Heber this afternoon. If next Sunday is fine Charlotte and I are going with Heber to Falkland. I came across a sermon of father's, "The Churchman's answer" and read it, also two of Uncle W.'s.

May 22 I finished my white crochet bonnet this morning as it rained too hard for me to go to drawing school. Louisa spent the evening at Mrs. Jones's with Charlotte. Miriam finished Mrs. Walker's bonnet that she has been making for her.

May 23 Miss Morrisey came today, quite unexpectedly to make my tan coloured dress which fits very well. She also did part of Tory's & Bella's. Mrs. Widden sent up Charley Wallace's daguerreotype for us to look at. A French steamer is now in the harbour and Aunt M. & Louisa saw two of them [sailors] in at Graham's where they found it impossible to make themselves understood. Cousin Ben sent me up a parcel that Aunt Eliza had enclosed to him for me which contained a sovereign in a purse, as my birthday present, accompanied by a very kind note. Mr. Rowley and Mr. Balfour came up in the evening. Mr. Balfour came first, and we had a very pleasant evening. Mr. Balfour said that they had been soldiering at a most alarming rate all day, practicing for tomorrow. Tomorrow is Charlotte's birthday as well as the Queen's. We heard the guns firing and as it brought down a cloud which happened to be overhead, we at first thought it was a thunder storm, but the regularity of the peals soon revealed our mistake, probably from the peculiar forms of the clouds. Each shot echoed around us, even until when we saw smoke as were hardly sure whence the smoke came.

May 24 Poor Charlotte has had but a bad birthday, for Uncle William and Heber both rose with a severe sick head ache. Her presents were a writing desk, fitted up, a brooch, a work box, and a Keble. Mrs. Jones & Mrs. McCulla came to spend the day. We went to the review. Heber & Mr. Rowley, Louisa, Miriam,

Bella, Tory and I. Charlie Almon joined us on the ground. I liked it very much, though we were entangled in a skirmishing party who shot us without mercy & I was almost deafened by the guns, or cannons. Mr. Boggs, Mr. Rowley & Dr. Munro came up in the evening, but Dr. Munro's visit was occasioned by an unfortunate accident. Fred, with the other boys, was firing off a small cannon in honor of the day, when having foolishly put a stone in it, it shot him in the leg. Dr. Munro says he cannot get the stone out tonight, but he will be up tomorrow morning. If it had gone an inch higher, he might have lost his leg. An invitation came to us from Addie Gore to go to a large party tomorrow night given to the officers of the French steamer. It is Ascension day, so we are not going.

May 25 &ep; Went to church three times. Dr. Munro came up with Dr. Bell to see Fred. They decided not to try for the stone, but to let it work itself out. I copied Mr. Jones's will for Heber to send to Mrs. Jones. Louisa says that the Gores want me very much, as there are but few ladies that can speak French very fluently. It is one month since Mr. Jones died.

May 26 &ep; Miss Morrisey came today and made Bella's & Tory's dresses & part of Aunt Mary's. Letters from home. They have not yet told me where they live, but most teasing allusions to their own home. Josey is at the bottom of it all and to punish her, I am going to keep back a number of letters which have been written will be [indecipherable] to her. I went down to Mrs. Robie's to tell Dawber about his mother. Coming back I got a couple of oranges for Fred and met Cousin Ben who walked up with me. Dr. Munro, who was at the Gore's last night, said I was very much missed as there was but one lady, Miss D. Dusueir, who could speak fluently. He gave us a very amusing account of the ball. Fred is doing very well.

May 27 &ep; Miss Morrisey again. She finished Aunt M's dress and made two muslins sacks for Tory & Bella. A great many callers came today. I have been reading to Fred until he fell asleep. I have also helped him to keep up with his French & Latin class-es. He is very anxious not to lose ground. I never knew any one more patient and anxious not to give trouble. I was sitting with him when Dr. Munro came today and made off in a great hurry, for I thought he was going to probe the wound.

"Chocolate Lake from Wood near its Head,"
Alexander Cavalié Mercer, 1842

"Three Mile Church"
1840-1846, unknown artist

Three Mile Church was located in the area
now known as Fairview,
a community on the outskirts of Halifax.

May 28 〜 Uncle William preached this morning and Mr. Maturin this afternoon. Heber went to Falkland. We were to have gone today, but it was too foggy. Drs. Munro & Bell came up today and have ordered poulticing for Fred. The Archdeacon preached tonight. I did not go.

May 29 〜 Drew and finished the piece I was drawing. It was one of Harding's, a shore scene. I am going to do another sea or shore piece next time. I bought a parasol at Duffus's & Tupper's as Aunt M.'s present to me and in the afternoon walked out with Miry & Heber to Falklands and the arm. It was a most lovely walk and one of the loveliest scenes I ever saw was at the head of a row of larches in front of Mr. Pryor's, just when were catch the first glimpse of Chocolate Lake, and the arm. Dr. Munro came up and spent the evening. Louisa sang, but I was too tired by my long walk.

May 30 〜 The wind today blew a perfect hurricane. I went down to draw and sketch in the piece I was to begin. There are several very nice figures in it. I was almost blown away coming home. The *Kingston* going out tomorrow, I finished my letters tonight and made a good many papers for the frame that, with Miry's assistance, I am making for Uncle Morton.

May 31 〜 I went down to draw, first going down the town with Bella to get some things we wanted. Met Dr. Munro. I shaded half of my picture. When I came home I found a message from Cousin Ben asking me to go out for a drive with him in the afternoon. So about three, or a little after, he came with a very pretty horse and wagon. We drove out to the Three Mile House and there round by Arch. Bishop Walsh's, out by Down's and up the road on the other side of the arm to the granite quarries. We reached home about six o'clock after a very pleasant drive. I heard Fred's Latin and went to church. I felt a little tired after my drive.

June 1 〜 Went down town with Charlotte and Louisa who were executing some commissions for Mr. Nichols. I bought a gingham dress at Duffus & Tupper's. Worked on Uncle Morton's leather work frame, which with Miry's help will be very pretty.

Andrew Downs with His Dogs, ca. 1870

Downs established a zoological gardens near the present site of the Armdale Rotary. Halifax residents often traveled to Downs' to see his exotic birds and animals, or to stroll through his wooded grounds. The grounds at Walton Cottage gardens, as Downs called his estate, were home to a vast number and species of birds, moose, deer, seals, and bears.

June 2   Mother's Wedding day. I went down to draw and when I came back varnished what Miry had done on my frame and stained my hands very much and as luck would have it, we are invited to Miss Murdock's tonight. I shall have to wear gloves, although it is a very small party [indecipherable]. Just back from the party. I am very tired. It was larger than I expected but very dull. Danced with C. Almon, A. Scott, T. Grigor, & was engaged to J. Twining, but came home before. I like A. Scott very much. He came home with me and C. Almon with Bella. We had half a doz. offers of escorts, M. Grassi, T. Grigor, M. Almon, T. Twining, Mr. Murdock, Mr. Saunders of the *Vestal*, besides those who came with us.

June 3   Miss Morrisey came to make Charlotte's & Miriam's dresses. I finished a white slip for myself. Dr. Munro called and was very pleasant they say, but I did not go down. He took Heber out fishing. The *Kingston* did not go out until today. Miss McKie came up to give me a lesson in sketching [indecipherable] the gallery. Young C. Charman came up to Bella's great honor.

June 4   White Sunday. The *Halifax* came in this morning without my knowing it, as the wind was so high that they could not put up the signal. So, I was very agreeably surprised when Heber brought me a letter. He was at the Citadel and so knew. I cannot have the parcels until tomorrow. Uncle W. went to Dartmouth this evening. Louisa with him. Finished the piece I was drawing and gave it to Heber. The wind was very high, but we went over to Dartmouth, Heber & Miry, and I and enjoyed it very much. This evening I rec'd the home parcels, consisting of boots, papers, Mrs. Wilkins's butter print, some capes for myself, a blue silk, a muslin, and a muslin de beige.

June 5   Went down to draw. Met Dr. Munro. Sketched in the piece I am to do of a group of children sliding. Finished the frame this afternoon. We were going to walk with Heber, but Dr. Munro called for him to go out driving with him and, as both Miry and I were tired, we were very glad. I have been writing home this evening.

June 7   ◈   Miss Morrisey came and made my silk dress. It is very becoming and fits nicely. Cousin Ben called today to take Miry out driving and she says she had a delightful time. I was very glad, for she has not had a drive for a long time. We went to church in the evening. Uncle W. preached.

June 8   ◈   Uncle W. came home at one o'clock with the news that Uncle Morton was in town. I thought it would be very pleasant to go under his escort and wrote him a note immediately asking him to let me. I was pretty sure he would not refuse for Mother's sake. So I began to pack up immediately and had made all my arrangements before he came. It rained so hard in the evening that I gave up expecting him, but he came about eight o'clock and said that he had come down in one wagon and would drive me up tomorrow. I was delighted. It is far pleasanter than to go in the coach. He saw all my drawings and thinks I improved rapidly. I am very glad. He says he cannot tell me exactly when we shall go, but not before twelve tomorrow. He gave me three pounds as I wanted to pay Miss McKie before I went.

June 9   ◈   I do not yet date Windsor. The Rail Road meeting kept Uncle Morton later than expected, and he came up for a few minutes to tell me. We are to go at ten tomorrow. Heber had brought me a beautiful bouquet to take with me and I have kept it in water to preserve it until tomorrow.

Dr. Munro came up to see Fred, and seeing my trunks in the hall found out that I was going. I went down to bid him goodbye. He said he was sorry I was going. Hoped to see me in Halifax again. I wrote home.

A Trip to Windsor and Cornwallis

Upon arriving in the Annapolis Valley, New England Planters and Loyalists inhabited valuable, fertile land originally farmed by the Acadians. These groups established township-like governments and town militia. They erected churches and built homes reminiscent of those they had left behind in New England, thus creating what must have been a strong sense of local identity shaping the character of the area.

Agriculture was one of the main pursuits of valley residents, but shipbuilding, driven by the need to transport produce and locally mined gypsum, was another significant industry. It would be several years following Sarah's visit that Windsor and the valley would be linked to the capital city by rail. Until then, Windsor was a half-day trip by carriage from Halifax.

Much of the history of the Windsor area is tied to King's College. Founded in 1789 by newly arrived Loyalists, it was a place of higher learning for the sons of privileged Nova Scotian families and a place of training for Anglican clergymen. An academy was also established as a private secondary school. Students lived in relative comfort in an on-campus residence and were permitted to have their personal servants reside with them.

The Baptist Church also played a significant role in the history of the valley. As the established church of Nova Scotia, the Anglican Church was generally the church of the upper classes. It excluded those from other religious backgrounds from attending its schools and generally situated its churches only in affluent areas. Not all Nova Scotians found this arrangement acceptable. In the late eighteenth century, Planter and evangelist Henry Alline travelled throughout rural Nova Scotia preaching the benefits of living a modest life—no drinking and no gambling. Devoted to John the Baptist, Alline took his preaching to many frontier communities that were geographically isolated from the church centres. The fallout from his preaching resulted in many of his converts joining the Baptist denomination. In 1838 the Baptists founded Acadia University, known then as Queen's University, to serve the growing Baptist population.

COLLEGIATE SCHOOL, WINDSOR, N. S.

Engraving of the Collegiate School, ca. 1869
King's Collegiate School or King's Academy served younger boys and was
located on the same campus as King's College.

The Annapolis Valley was the ancestral home to many of
Nova Scotia's most influential families, such as the Haliburtons
and the Uniackes; it was also a summer retreat for fashionable city-
dwellers. Members of the legislative assembly who represented valley ridings normally maintained homes in the city and in their riding. While in the valley, they kept busy social calendars, took long
drives in the country, and picnicked with friends. The valley was
also home to some of the most successful farms in the province.
Loyalist families such as the Starrs of Starr's Point, who resettled
the lush farms established by the deported Acadians, often found
themselves the owners of very profitable farms. Others who had
received large land grants succeeded in tenant farming.

The Annapolis Valley was Sarah's ancestral home and home to
many family members, old friends, and acquaintances of her
mother and father. The Cunninghams (her mother's family) were
successful gypsum merchants and landowners with vast holdings,
including the Wentworth Estate (originally the Winkworth
Estate), Saulsbrook Farm, and numerous smaller farms and gypsum quarries. John Cunningham immigrated from Ireland as a
young man, arriving in Halifax with his family in the late 1760s.
In 1771 he was appointed Commissioner of Indian Affairs. Upon

John Cunningham's death, his estate was divided among his three children, but it was his son Richard who continued to build the family's real estate in the Windsor area. Richard married Sarah Wentworth Morton, the daughter of the Hon. Perez and Sarah Morton and great niece of Lady Wentworth, at the summer estate of the Prince of Wales in 1809. Richard purchased the vast Saulsbrook Farm from its original owner, Thomas Saul, a Halifax merchant. Located on present-day Chester Road, the estate became the Cunningham family home. Richard was also the owner of the former Winkworth estate, built by Winkworth Tonge, which he renamed Wentworth in honour of his wife's heritage. Sections of the land owned by Richard contained gypsum deposits which he began mining and leasing to miners for a portion of the profits. Other sections of the Cunningham estate supported more than ten tenant farms, which during Richard's lifetime were profitable. In 1830, Richard died, and the administration of his vast estate passed to his son Perez Morton Cunningham, who at the time was training to be a lawyer.

"Kings College Campus," ca.1870

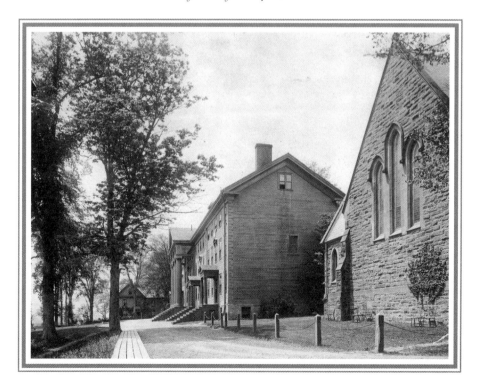

Sarah's maternal grandparents, Sarah
Apthorp Morton and Richard Cunningham,
were married at the Duke of Kent's country
residence on August 22, 1809. Sarah's grand-
mother was the niece of Lady Frances
Wentworth. Lady Wentworth and her husband, Governor Sir John Wentworth, were
the first residents of Government House.

Morton, his sisters Griselda, Eliza, Frances, and Charlotte, and brother John were raised on the Saulsbrook Estate in Windsor. The family was known to be very social and often hosted professors from King's College. Morton continued to live at Saulsbrook with his mother until her death in 1849. He then began living with Reginald Porter, a good friend from his years at King's College. Together Morton Cunningham and Reginald Porter founded a law practice, and their shared accommodations became known locally as "Bachelor Hall." Eventually the two men took separate homes close together in the town of Windsor.[1]

Frances Sarah Wentworth Cunningham married the Rev. John Storrs in 1841, also at the summer estate of the Prince of Wales. Frances died childless just two years later. In 1844 John Storrs married Melanie Hayne and they had at least four children: John, Mary Jane, Robert, and Arthur. Rev. John Storrs was the rector of St. John's Church in Cornwallis, and he and his family lived nearby in a large rectory; he operated a small farm and remained close to the Cunningham family. It was with John Storrs and his second wife that Sarah stayed during her time in Cornwallis (now Port Williams). Sarah divided her stay in the Annapolis Valley between Windsor and Cornwallis. Mrs. Wilkins, who had been a friend of Sarah's mother, kindly invited Sarah and her cousin Louisa (Bullock) to stay with her in Windsor. The invitation was fortunate for Sarah, as she wanted to visit her family in Windsor but it could not have been stayed with her unmarried uncle. The Wilkins family was also very influential and known for their social gatherings, ensuring that Sarah and Louisa were invited to the most distinguished Windsor social events during their visit.

St. John's Anglican Church, Cornwallis, ca. 1920

St. John's Anglican Church—the parish church—was
established in 1810. Sarah's uncle Rev. John Storrs was
named its rector in 1841, a position he held until 1876.

"Ten women and four men in evening dress,"
Emma Haliburton, 1840–1842

Windsor and Cornwallis

June 10   Windsor. Uncle Morton came up at little after ten and we started. It has been a most glorious day and the happiest since I first left home, happy as the winter has been. Uncle Morton told me everything we passed and stopped when we came to any-thing particularly pretty or interesting. We stopped at the half-way house to lunch and change horses for Uncle M. did not bring his own horses. We had a delicious lunch and I never enjoyed a drive so much. I hope Uncle Morton enjoyed it too. We did not get in until about six, for Uncle M. did not hurry, but drove slowly and stopped now & then to so show me different things. Aunt E. says he is taciturn but he found plenty to say to me. He says he will take me himself to Saulsbrook. We met Lady at the door and Uncle M. left me with her to establish myself for a day or two. He will drive me up to Cornwallis if he has time. Aunt Eliza came up as soon as she heard of my arrival. She has not altered much except that she has grown very fat. Mr. W. came down from H.- he did not get here till twelve o'clock as he had obtained no delays on the road. I did not feel in the least tired until I got out of the carriage and began to rest myself. Then I found that I was very tired for the roads are rough. But Uncle Morton kept me so interested all the way that I did not feel it before. Mrs. Wilkins is very kind. I have such a pleasant room and the bed looks so inviting that it being after twelve, I must go. I wrote to Miss McKie, as I had not time to bid her good-bye.

June 11   🖎   I woke at five, but did not rise until six. Wrote home and to Aunt Mary. Went to church. Mrs. McKay called for me in her carriage as the church where we go in the morning is at some distance. Mr. Gilpin does not read well as he is almost blind, but I like his preaching.[2] Mr. Harry King came up & spoke to me, and his daughter Harriet.[3] It rained very hard in the night and everything looks so fresh and beautiful. I have come to bed quite early as I feel still tired.

June 12   🖎   A most lovely day. I woke, as yesterday, at five but did not rise for some time after six, for my shoulders and neck ached as if my head were too heavy for them. That is where I feel most tired. I wrote a good deal before breakfast. Mrs. G. Wilkins & Mrs. Forman called. Mr. Wilkins went to Halifax about two o'clock. Harriet King called to say that her mother was going away tomorrow and was very anxious to have me spend the evening there. And I asked her to take a walk with me. While I was putting on my things, Uncle Morton came to see if I was ready to go to Cornwallis, but hearing of Miss King's invitation, kindly said he would take me tomorrow at ten. Harriet and I went out and passed by Uncle M's house and round by Clifton over the covered bridge and back by Uncle M's office. We met Arthur Haliburton, who said he had been to call on me and was very sorry that I was not at home. He said he had heard from Halifax. When I reached home I found that I had had four more calls, three daughters of Harry King and the daughter of Weaton King. In the afternoon Mrs. McKay sent me an invitation to drive with her. Sarah King also was invited and went. We reached home again a little after six and I dressed for Mrs. King's. I wore my silk for the first time. We had a very pleasant evening. Bessie King enticed me to let her curl my hair round my face which she said was a marked improvement. We did not stay late but have been talking to Mrs. Wilkins some time since I came home. I intended to pack my trunk before I went to bed but I am too tired. I shall have plenty of time in the morning.

June 13   I rose early and had my trunk about half packed when Aunt Eliza kindly came to help me. I was very glad for I was in need of assistance. She folded my things beautifully and packed them as if she were used to it. My head ached sadly. Uncle Morton came about ten. I forgot to say yesterday that he passed while we were waiting for Mrs. McKay and told us about John Napier, an old servant at Saulsbrook. Mr. Porter came up while he was speaking to us, and Uncle M. introduced him to me. Driving to Cornwallis today, on entering the bridge, Uncle M. introduced Willie Jon to me, or rather me to him, as he was father's old servant in college. Uncle M. told me that Mr. Porter had bought Dr. Mountovaue's house and was going to live there next month. I do not know how they will ever live separate. They say Mr. Porter is going to marry, but that may be a report arising from his having taken this house. We had a pleasant drive. The Horton Mts. are most beautiful, but I am afraid I was a rather stupid companion, my head ached so. Uncle Morton let me drive part of the way to teach me and he says I would soon learn to drive very well. He staid to dinner at Uncle Storrs' and about two hours after to rest himself. Uncle Storrs is very kind indeed and his wife & children very pretty, genuinely. Melanie & John are not so pretty as the three younger ones, but they are all very good. Mrs. Storrs is much smaller and prettier than I had expected, for I had heard that her health was poor. I played a little after Uncle Morton had gone, they have a very good piano, in excellent tune. In the evening, Uncle Storrs showed me his garden and farm and we sat the verandah for a while to enjoy the cool evening air, but were driven into the house by the mosquitoes. My room is very pleasant. I walked down the town a little way with Uncle S. this evening.

June 14   Uncle Storrs drove us to Kentville and leaving Mrs. Storrs at the Rand's, we went in to Beech Hill from which there is a most magnificent view. Unfortunately the tide was out so that I did not see it in its full beauty but I was charmed & delighted with what I did see. He went to see a young woman who was to be baptized, named Crow and she had a sweet little baby. On our return we called at Mrs. Harris' and Mrs. Rand's where we lunched and accepted an invitation there for next Tuesday. They are coming to us on Friday. After a little shopping we came home by a different way, very beautiful but not so pretty I thought as the one by which we went. I wrote home, as Mrs. Harris is going and offered to take my letters for me. I wrote to Miriam & Charlotte by post as Saturday is Miriam's birthday & if I post the letter tomorrow it will just reach her in time. Sewed a little.

June 15   Went to Kentville to post my letters. Stopped to visit a family named Hall who knew mother and her family. They are very queer people indeed. They knew Mother's family well and I believe the Misses Hall went to school with Mother and Aunt Charlotte. We received a message from the Rands, saying that friends coming to stay with them would prevent them from coming to us on Friday. I heard Mary Jane read and went out in the evening to see Uncle Storrs mow a little.

June 16   The first loud thunder I have heard in Nova Scotia. One flash was very bright & from the report that immediately followed, evidently struck at not great distance. Uncle Storrs came home this evening and read a man was struck on Beech Hill and very much injured, but not killed. There fell a most refreshing rain all day until near night. I wrote, read, sewed, and played. Uncle Storrs was at the request of old Mr. Hall, looking up the opinions of different commentaries upon the passage from St. Paul's sermon to the Athenians. " I perceive that in all things ye are too superstitious." I think it means too ready to embrace any new religion without sufficiently caring whether it be true or not. A fault not confined to the Athenians, or even the earlier ages of Christianity.

June 17 A most brilliant morning but very windy. The children were writing to Aunt Eliza in hopes of an opportunity and I wrote too, to be ready if a chance should occur. Uncle Starr went down to the post office but came back empty handed, somewhat to my disappointment. I had hoped to have celebrated Miriam's birthday by enjoying letters. Uncle Storrs took us for a drive as I thought and called upon Miss Norris and then at a Mr. Starr's where we left Mrs. Storrs, to go to Mrs. Prescott's, nearly next door. On our return to Mr. Starr's I found, to my surprise, that we were to spend the afternoon and take tea there. I was hardly prepared for such an event, but bore it very philosophically by going to take a very pleasant walk with Martha, the youngest of the two sisters. We had a pleasant evening and came home immediately after tea. Mrs. Prescott invited us to dinner on Monday. I tore my dress in my walk and have made my eyes ache mending it by candle light.

June 18 I went to Cornwallis to church this morning and Melanie and I accompanied Uncle Storrs to Wolfville in the afternoon. It looked very much like rain and smelt very much like smoke, when we came out of church. A Mrs. Starr asked us to go to her house near-by, while Uncle Storrs was seeing about the horse.[4] She knew mother and father long ago, and invited us to dinner next Thursday. We drove home very quickly in fear of rain. Met a colt on the way home which had nearly hung itself in an old horse's harness.

June 19 I sewed nearly all the morning. Was not up as early as usual. We went to the Prescott's to dinner and came away after an early tea. Mr. R.P. said he was going to Windsor tomorrow and if I had any commands. So, I said I should have liked to send a note to Uncle Morton, but had not it with me. So he offered me the use of his desk and I wrote to ask him to come for me next Monday because Uncle Storrs does not know whether or not Bessie Rand will be married then. It will be very soon certainly. Mr. Prescott was at S. Boston two years ago and as soon as he mentioned it I remembered him perfectly. Uncle S. seemed quite astonished at his offer of the desk and says it is not often that Robert Prescott is so courteous.[5] I am very glad the exception is in my favor, for I was anxious to get a note to Uncle Morton. Mrs. D. Allison, Mrs. Scott & Miss Norris were there, besides ourselves. Miss Hammell, a sister of Mrs. Prescott, resides in the house. Mrs. Sate is suffering from a goiter. She is the first person I ever saw with one. I wore my tan colored dress. It was quite foggy when we came home. There is a report of a large fire between Annapolis & Liverpool, another of St. Johns being of fire, another that is at Miramishe.

June 20   I finished that long waiting skirt and was very glad of it. Uncle Storrs had a note from C. Allison asking him to marry them on Friday after next so I wrote to Uncle Morton to tell him that he need not come for me. James Parsons, Uncle S's tenant brought me a parcel from Kentville, containing a letter for Aunt Eliza, one from Heber one from Louisa, and the Habit skirt she was making me. So I answered them immediately, in order to take advantage to our going to Kentville this evening to post them. We started about four. I wore my blue silk. We found that they had expected us some time before. Uncle Storrs went on to Beech Hill to see the Mrs. Crow he went to see before. Rebecca has had another note from Miry, and told me about it. We had strawberries for tea, the first in any quantity that I had seen. We came away about ten, and I never drove in such a dark night in my life, and going a great part of the way through the woods made it much darker. To add to it all, they had not been mending the roads. It was impossible to see the horse's head and could only tell when the road lay by the numerous glow worms on the banks at the side. I never saw so many in my life before and uneasy as I was I could not help admiring them. Two or three times Uncle S. had to get out and lead the horse. Hector is very careful and well used to the road, but several times we got into the ditch or up on the bank. When we reached home Uncle S. acknowledged that he had never driven in such a dark night before. He would not say so before we got home, for Mrs. S. was so frightened. We were an hour coming home. Uncle Storrs eyes trouble him a little from straining to see.

June 21   I rose very early. Finished the handkerchief that has been lying by so long. My head ached very much, so I did not go out driving today, but wrote home and heard the children's

Christ Church, Windsor, ca. 1890

*Completed in 1790, Christ Church serves
as the parish church.*

lessons. We had a strawberry supper. A Mr. Sam Starr and his nephew came to put up a new pig pen for Uncle Storrs.

June 22 ～ Uncle S. was writing to St. John N.B. so I slipped in a note to Fanny. It is the first time I have written her since I have been in N.S. I sewed this morning and we set off to Mrs. Starr's, stopping at one or two shops on the way. While Mrs. S. was in one shop, Uncle S. and I made a call on old Mrs. Barrs, a daughter of Judge DeWolfe, where father and mother used to stay.[6] We had a pleasant afternoon. Saw the Prescotts returning from Windsor and stopping at the P.O. on our return. Learned that Mr. R. P. had taken Uncle's letters on with him. We received them from the toll keeper and also one for me from Uncle Morton, which Mr. Prescott had brought.

June 23 ～ We drove to Kentville and on our return, by a road I had never been before; through the woods to Conor St. and so home by the dike road. Uncle S. said we had driven about fourteen miles. Mrs. Scott, Mrs. Allison & Miss Norris came to tea. I like Miss Norris very much. Worked a little on my cloak. Been reading "The Maiden & the Married Life of May Powell, afterwards Mistress Milton."

June 24 ～ Rode to Wolfville with Uncle Storrs. Went up the way behind Acadia College from which there is a delightful view. As Mr. Sonter was coming to dinner, we had not time to go as far as we wished, i.e. to a place further on the Mountain which commands a view of the Gaspereau. Stopped at the P.O. and received a letter from Heber enclosing one from home. They want me to be at home before the last of July. I do not know how I can, but it seems very selfish not to wish to. Mr. Sonter came up just as we turned away from the office and walked up with us. He speaks very broad Scottish and is rather pleasant. He went away before ten and Uncle Storrs, Melanie & I walked up to the hill, which gives a pretty view of the church & parsonage. When we came home I read aloud to Uncle S. until nearly twelve and then had some strawberries and went to bed.

June 25 ～ Every one overslept themselves this morn-ing. I went to Wolfville to church in the morning & to Cornwallis in the afternoon. Wrote home.

June 26 🖎 I returned to Windsor today. Uncle Storrs brought me back by the old post road as I had never seen it. It is incomparably prettier than the new one, particularly the Gaspereau valley and the Horton Mts. The scene of Evangeline; Longfellow did well to immortalize such a lovely spot. It surpasses in beauty any thing I ever saw. Not so much grandeur as the Cornwallis Valley possesses with Blomidon and the rest of that range for a background, but in peaceful, quiet, Sunday-like loveliness, I can hardly imagine anything to surpass it. In Windsor I found an invitation awaiting me from Mrs. Gilpin to go to tea.[7] Dr. Gray was there, but I was too tired. So in the evening Dr. Gray came up purposely to see me. He brought his younger son Henry with him. Henry is invited to stay at Mrs. Wilkins's while he is in town. He is a pleasant, gentlemanly boy, but not nearly so handsome or sensible as Cousin Ben. Dr. Fraser came in in the evening. Thinks I look like mother. I went out and bought a few trifles for Mrs. Storrs and the children, for Uncle Storrs to take home tomorrow.

June 27 🖎 Uncle Storrs went home today. I saw Uncle Morton for half a minute only as I was on my way to church to see Augusta Haliburton married. Louisa, Heber, and Uncle William came up in the coach. Mr. Cunard and Mr. Halliburton called before they came. Cousin Ben came in and I wanted to telegraph to Halifax for some forgotten music and dresses and he offered to go with me, as I did not know where the office was. After dispatching that, he asked me to take a walk with him and I was content and went much to the edification of Andy Uniacke & Lewis Bliss and Charlie Gore. I forgot to say that Charlie came up in the coach and is going to stay at Mrs. Wilkins's too, so there is a houseful. Andy Uniacke thinks Cousins very convenient titles. Returning we met Heber and Uncle William who joined us up to Ferry Hill which I had not yet seen. Cousin Ben had to leave at three as he had some business to do in town. Bland Sawyer was with us. Heber broke off a piece of petrified shell or shells bedded in petrified earth. He is going to take them to Morton.

June 28 🖎 I went to Uncle M's office to get some money as I had to buy a dress. Heber and Louisa were with me and went into the office at Uncle M's invitation. I bought my dress at Allison's. There was a dinner party at Mrs. Wilkin's. The Andrew Uniacke's, The H. Kings, Mrs. McKay, Aunt Eliza, Dr. & Henry Gray & ourselves made twelve. Dr. Montivani and R. Halliburton

Sophia Almon, ca. 1870

Sophia was the wife of Mather Byles Almon and daughter of John Pryor, (merchant and MLA). The couple had fourteen children, including Charlie. Mather attended King's College and became a merchant, an insurance agent, one of the founders of the Bank of Nova Scotia, a governor of Dalhousie University and King's College, and a member of the Legislative and Executive councils. Mather and Sophia were involved in many Halifax charities and were devoted members of St. Paul's Church congregation.

Rev. Dr. George McCawley, D.D., ca. 1870

McCawley was a Church of England priest and teacher. He received his early education at King's College, Windsor, later taught at King's College, Fredericton and was chaplin to the Legislative Council of New Brunswick. During this time he married Anne Odell and they had one daughter. In 1836 McCawley was appointed president of King's College and held the position until 1875.

came in in the afternoon for a short time. Uncle W. and Heber dined here. Mrs. C. Wilkins called.

June 29

Mrs. McCulla came up and cut my dress, leaving me barely time to get ready for the exercises. Mrs. Wilkins and I drove with Mrs. McKay. Louisa went with Lady and Charlie Gore. Heber met us and found us seats. We should otherwise have had some difficulty, as it was almost late and unusually full. The exercises, as far as I was able to judge were particularly excellent. Norman Uniacke quite astonished me by his English composition. After it was over, Dr. McCawley invited us to a collation in his house which proved a most delicious one and acceptable also, after the mental first. The collation ended, the bishop escorted Mrs. Almon to the library and invited Louisa and me to go too.

Heber and Louisa Almon followed. We afterwards went into Henry Almon's room which proved to be the one which father, Uncle Morton and Trimingham had occupied. When we came

Mrs. Anne McCawley, ca. 1870 Anne McCawley was the daughter of William Franklin Odell, New Brunswick provincial secretary. She married Rev. George McCawley, President of King's College, Windsor.

out, we encountered Cousin Ben and Charlie Almon who joined us in an excursion to the roof of the college, which is flat and commands a most magnificent view. Unfortunately the roof is covered with filth, and the day being entirely warm, we struck most perseveringly and could hardly tear ourselves away. We walked home after having had an encounter of wits with R. Haliburton, who thought fit to sneer at a girl, knowing Latin. He would not have known that I know anything of it, if Louisa had not told him. In the afternoon, all had gone out for a walk but me, and I being tired, preferred lying down as we were to go to a party at Mrs. McCawley's in the evening. Cousin Ben came into the house & called me, so I went down, and he said he was very tired and wanted to know if I would not play for him. The parlor was quite dark and cool, so he went in and lay down upon the sofa and I played and talked to him when suddenly in walked Mrs. Wilkins and three navy officers. She threw open the shutters and there we were. The officers being strangers did not know of any relationship between us and there was a laugh at our expense. My great trouble was that my back hair being very rough, as I had been lying down. But I faced the enemy and kept my hair in its proper place, in the background. We went to Mrs. McCawley's in the evening in Mrs. McKay's carriage. In opening the carriage door, Thomas slipped and fell directly in front of the wheels and by the horse's heels. The horse started and I do not know what would have become of us it had not been for Arthur who stopped the horse and extricated Thomas. We spent a very pleasant evening. I danced with Robie Uniacke, Norman Uniacke, and some one else. Charlie Gore, Lewis Bliss, and several others asked me, but there were but three quadrilles and I was engaged. Once I danced vis a vis to Mr. Sullivan, one of the navy officers of the Morning. Thomas came so late that we were just on the point of giving him up and walking home. We had plenty of escorts to have made a pleasant walk. Heber, Cousin Ben, Charlie Gore, Charlie Almon, Lewis Bliss, Andy & Robie Uniacke &c. but we were tired enough to be well pleased with driving. As we descended the hill near Uncle Morton's we came into a thick fog, not more than 10 feet high so decided that we saw the horse enter it before we did. Dr. Gray, Uncle W. & Heber dined at Mr. Wilkins's.

Fort Lawrence, Windsor, ca. 1955
The blockhouse was part of a larger military base; today, only the blockhouse—the oldest surviving blockhouse in North America—remains.

Clifton, ca. 1890

This is Clifton, the home of T.C. Haliburton and his family, somewhat as Sarah would have known it; the roof had yet to be expanded and the driveway still passed in front of the house.

June 30   We were very tired last night and did not rise very early this morning. Uncle W. went home this afternoon. The Bishop called today to bid good-bye. So did the Pryors, Pikes and Almons. Cousin Ben asked us to make him a bouquet to send to St. John's by the steamer but it did not come in tonight as was expected. We were invited to Gerrish Hall but were engaged to Mr. Harry King's. Dr. McCawley was there. Louisa had a long and apparently pleasant conversation with him. I sang, by particular request, some Latin songs father had written for me, which provided considerable amusement among the young collegians.

July 1   Heber and the Pryors are in despair at the non-arrival of the steamer. To console them we (Louisa, the Misses Pyke, Heber & I) walked up to the fort, which commands a very pretty view. We could see Wentworth (old Winkworth), which is Uncle Morton's great pleasure producing estate. I believe Uncle W. came back from Halifax yesterday eve where he went, either Wednesday evening or Thursday morn. Mrs. Wilkins had a dinner party. Heber was invited, but went back to Halifax in despair of the steamer arrival. Mr. C. Wilkins came in in the evening and I was playing. He came and sat down by the piano and talked about Uncle Morton a good deal. Aunt M., Louisa & I called this afternoon at Clifton and Gerrish Hall. The grounds around Clifton are very beautiful but we did not get in. The garden at Gerrish Hall is in its glory. We brought away some most beautiful roses, but the morning was the pleasantest part of the day. We did not breakfast until ten and Mr. Wilkins repeated poetry, principally Childe Harold, until twelve. He recites it so beautifully and with such feeling. This evening after all the company had gone, he did the same and sang to us Morris melodies until nearly twelve. It is not quite 12 and I am tired.

July 2   We walked home from church over the college fields and came out by Clifton. The wind was so high that it broke my parasol. Mr. Wilkins showed us a curious formation of land called the Punch Bowl from its shape. I wrote home a little.

July 3   Mr. Wilkins went to Halifax. We were invited to the Bliss's cottage for the afternoon, and Mrs. King's in the evening.[8] We picked strawberries at the cottage and amused ourselves in the long grass and picked bouquets in the garden. Mr. McKay took Harriet King and me for a short drive after we left the cottage. Charlie Gore drove and I sat in front with him. He drove very well. We had a very pleasant evening at Mrs. King's. Robie Uniacke walked us home.

Martock House, ca. 1865
Martock was built in 1840 by Col. E.K.S. Butler, who named the estate after his hometown in England. The area just south of Windsor thereafter became known as Martock.

Fourth of July!   We were up early, and the boys came to bid us good-bye as they were going in the coach; Robie, Norman & Andy Uniacke, Lewis Bliss & Charlie Gore. Mr. Hedgeson came from Saulsbrook on purpose to see me. Uncle Morton stopped for a moment to say he would take us to Saulsbrook today and stayed an hour. We sang to him and gave him some roses. Aunt E. brought me a letter from Uncle Storrs and an invitation for this evening from Mr. McKay, who afterwards sent Mr. W one for Uncle M & Mr. Porter, which I begged to carry. Fortunately there was no one in the office so I stayed there some little time. Uncle M. called for us at three, I sat behind as Louisa was more of a stranger than I. We passed before Saulsbrook and round by Martock entering the private road through Saulsbrook, between the hills and the cultivated part of the property, then turning, we drove up through the two smaller farms, through the belt of firs, and through the estate coming out at a little distance from the house itself. Uncle M. evidently did not wish to go to it, but at my request he turned and drove up to it, pointed out all that he thought would interest me & then we came away. There is a most magnificent belt of willows just beyond the orchard and continuing across the road. The finest, I think I ever saw. The estate is far more extensive than I thought it was, including part of the Ardoise Hills, which are very well wooded and very beautiful. Coming back, Uncle M. took us to the tops of Prospect, whence we saw the crest of Blomidon rising above the Horton Hills at a distance of more than twelve miles in a straight line. It is really a most extraordinary formation, being the end of a range running from the bay of Minas to St. Mary's Bay with only the interval of Digby Gut, which is evidently produced by some convulsion of nature, perhaps the deluge. It is almost perpendicular.

Returning, Uncle Morton took us to his own house, as we had never been there, and welcomed us to it most cordially. I ransacked the house, much to Louisa's pretended horror, but I think she was well pleased all the time, as she would not otherwise have seen half as much of the house as she did. Among other things, I brought to light a (so-called) portrait of Uncle Morton, but looked so little like him that I asked him who it was. After declining strawberries, which we offered, we returned home at half past seven, as we had to be at Mr. McKay's at eight. There was a withered bouquet on the mantelpiece and I told him he should have a better one tomorrow. We had a pleasant evening at Mrs. McKay's but I feel tired. Uncle Morton did not come & I was glad he did not, for Dr.

Fraser and Mr. King were the only gentlemen among more than 20 ladies. They congratulated me on its being the "Glorious Fourth".

July 5   We rose early and Louisa made a very handsome bouquet entirely of roses, and at nine o'clock, before anyone was up except the servants, we started to take it to Uncle Morton. L. would not go to the house, so she walked towards Clifton, while I took it. I could not make the bell ring, as the wire was stretched, so I went round through the garden and round to the back door and finally made the servant come. She looked rather astonished, but took the flowers and my message and let me out through the front door. I rejoined Louisa and after a pleasant, but warm walk, we returned home in full time for breakfast. We received an invitation to Gerrish Hall for the evening. It was very warm but we undertook to return some calls that must be returned, and went over the fields to Mrs. McCawley's, then to Mrs. Gilpin's then Miss Cochran's, Mrs. Rector King's, Dr. Montiavni's, Dr. Harding's, Misses Tonge's, and then home, perfectly exhausted. At Mrs. McCawley's, the first thing they did was to offer us both fans and then red wine and water, we looked so warm. The thermometer was 98° in the shade, but I felt it far more than much greater heat in Boston. We passed a very pleasant evening in the Hall and Dr. Fraser walked home with us. It was a very pleasant walk indeed.

July 6 ⇜ Miss Cochran came up this morning to invite us to spend the evening there. Just after she went, Uncle Morton came in. I was bewailing having to come home with Mr. Cochran for escort, and to our amazement Uncle M. said he would be happy to call for us and walk home with us. Louisa and I went over the bridge for a walk and Willie Jon refused to take any toll. We called at Uncle M's office on the way and sat with him for a little while. He gave me *Nicholas Nickleby* which he had bought for me. Mrs. McKay sent her carriage for us and Aunt Eliza to go down and it was ordered to return for us a little after ten, as we did not think Uncle M. was in earnest. The evening was not very pleasant as we were too tired to enjoy ourselves much. There was no one there besides ourselves and the Misses Tonge. To our great pleasure as well as surprise, Uncle M. came for us punctually at a little after ten and the surprise almost took away Miss Cochran's breath. The carriage did not come as soon as it was ordered and we all started to walk together, but meeting it on the road, Aunt E. and the Misses Tonge got in and drove home. I was very tired so we walked quite slow. We did not reach home until after eleven. I am almost sure we passed Mr. Porter on the road.

July 7 ⇜ This morning Louisa and I were sitting at the window when Uncle Morton came up and gave me a letter from Fanny. Mrs. Wilkins asked him to come up to tea and bring Mr. Porter. He said he would if possible. Later, I went over to his office to ask him for some money, but there were a good many people in the office, so he said he would come up, and he brought me some and gave it to me in the garden where I went to pick a rose for him. In the afternoon we drove out to Martock to call upon Mrs. Butler. It is a pretty place out there, just beyond Saulsbrook. Dr. Fraser called at Mrs. Wilkins' this morning and was being curious about Uncle Morton's going for us last night. He seemed to think it the most wonderful thing that had ever happened in Windsor. We waited tea until nine o'clock but Uncle M. did not come and we sat down without him. Mr. McKay was here and went to sleep while Louisa was singing some Italian songs and on waking up, thanked her for her beautiful music. We had some ice cream and cake and then Mr. McKay went home and we all dispersed to our rooms.

July 8 ⇜ We had a cold bath this morning and feel very much refreshed by it. Mrs. Wilkins received a telegraph from

Mr. Wilkins saying that he would come down tonight, but not until late. Harriet King and Madame Montivani called. I went out with Sady for a walk and went over a dyke. We met an Indian woman from whom I ordered a nest of boxes. I tore my dress and Aunt Eliza offered to mend it for me if I would first go to see a Miss Leonard, who formerly sewed for Mother. While she mended it, I went into the garden and made a bouquet for Uncle Morton which I took to him after dinner, with some more roses. He was not at home, but I arranged them in water on the table and came back again. Louisa says that Mr. Porter passed eleven times yesterday and seven today, while she was at the window.

July 9 ✑ Mr. Wilkins came home late last night, Mrs. McKay sent her carriage to take us to church early and came back for her. Mr. Wilkins walked. Mrs. W. was not very well and did not go at all. We walked home and suffered very much from the intense heat. Mr. Wilkins says that there is a very large fire near the half way house and that at times yesterday it was dangerous to pass. This afternoon Louisa & I alone went to church. Mr. W. is going away at two in the morning as he must be in town before ten.

July 10 ✑ Mr. Wilkins went about two and Mr. Wilkins sent a telegraph to say that he reached town at nine and dry, which we feared would not have been the case as it was raining hard through the night. I rec'd a telegraph from Uncle Storrs to say that he ought expect us tomorrow. Uncle Morton promised to take us and I went over to ask him if it would be perfectly convenient. He said it would, but he would not take us to the Academy today as he had hoped, but he would try to when we came back from Cornwallis. I did not feel well at all today, but called upon the King's. We went to Mr. McKay's to dinner where I tasted green peas for the first time this season. There is a York & Lancaster rose in her garden which came from Saulsbrook and I am going to ask Uncle Morton to get a slip of it for Mother. I looked all through the library for an architectural term and found it for Uncle Morton. Mrs. McKay played us for this evening and Dr. Fraser came in.

July 11 ✑ Uncle Morton came for us at ten. Louisa sat in front with him and I behind. We had a very pleasant drive indeed. Uncle Morton says he will get the horse from Mr. McKay and will take us to the Academy when we come back. I amused them when we reached Wolfville with the amount of local knowledge I had picked up on my previous visit here. Uncle Morton stayed to dinner and just before dinner, who should drive up the road with a very pretty pair of horses, but Mr. Prescott. He did not come in to dinner, but stayed in the parlor until we dined. While Uncle Morton was looking after his horse, Mr. P. invited us to come over before the cherries were gone, as he had some very fine trees. Just as Uncle Morton was going away he stopped his horse and said "It is very dusty and disagreeable in the coach, if it does rain, I will come for you." That was very pleasant indeed, so Louisa and I are looking forward with much pleasure to it. In the evening, as we were to be here so short a time, Uncle Storrs asked us if we were too tired to take a short drive. We said no and drove over the dyke leading back from the parsonage, over across the village on to the Wellington dyke, and so home. About six or seven miles which in addition to the twenty-two from Windsor made us feel quite ready for bed.

July 12 It rained heavily all the morning and Louisa and I sewed and sang, though we were sorry to lose even a day of our stay, it is already so short. About one o'clock it stopped raining and tho' still showery, we determined to venture. By the time we were ready, even the showers had ceased, and we set out. Uncle Storrs did not tell us where we were to go, but we came out by a road I had never been before, to the saw-mills, and then on till to our great surprise, we found ourselves at the base of the Blomidon range, about twenty or twenty five miles to the west of Blomidon itself. It was Master's Mountain, the easiest ascent on the range, but if that is the easiest, I should be sorry to ascend the steepest, we drove on the tops of the range for about seven miles, and came down the Ilsley Mountain where Louisa and I insisted on walking down, it was so steep, and it was well we did, for even with only Uncle Storrs in the wagon the horse fairly slid for two or three yards in one place before he could regain his footing and even walking down I found fatigued me more than walking six times the distance on level ground or even a moderate slope, would have done. I was surprised to see the top of the mt. so broad. It is about four miles wide on an average through the whole range. About half way up the Master's Mt. we stopped to look back upon the lost glorious scene I even beheld. The Cornwallis Valley being below us with the Horton Hills beyond, looking from the height at which we were almost as level as the valley between. The Hills were in brilliant sunshine, while through the valley so near the ground that it was perfectly black from the dense shade, moved a long heavy mass of cloud, looking every moment as if the next would see it settling down actually upon the ground. Nor were we far wrong for presently a part of it sank a little and appeared to drop down fringes or feelers and then it pelted so hard, that it looked like a steam or smoke. The rest sailed on as heavy and black as ever the Mts. beyond being, as we were still in sunshine and here and there parts of the valley. There was a very thick fog in the Bay, but still we could see a little land on the opposite side. The settlement at the foot of the Ilsley Mt. is Billtown.[9]

July 13   This morning being fine, Uncle Storrs proposed a lunch at eleven, and then starting for the mts. He is going to take us up the easiest road that there is up the Mt. to Blomidon. There is more nearer than four miles.[sic] It is called the Scotch Bay Road and the first half of it is not at all a difficult ascent, but the upper half is nothing but a bed of great, sharp, cornered rocks. I only wonder Hector did not cut his hoof off. But it is an exceedingly pretty road and the view above perfectly magnificent. It has the water view, which was wanting from the Masters & Ilsley mts. It commands a very fine view of the Basin of Minas and the mouth of the Windsor River. It is so high that we can see the tops of some of the Ardoise Hills, over the Horton range. "Hills rise o'er hills" I had no idea that the valley was so very extensive, or that it contains so much thick, apparently unpeneratable forest. It is the most extensive once I ever saw. We had to get out of the carriage and walk about a mile to an open space on the very edge of the hill, a perfect precipice, where tops of the nearest trees were far below us. The part of the valley immediately below us is called Pereau but the most flourishing place we passed though was a little ship-building village called Habitant. We descended from the Mt. by the Old Scotch Bay Road, upon which the one we came up is an improvement. It was so very steep that Uncle S. said that with any other horse he would have wished to walk down, but that as it was, he would rather have us stay in the carriage as we could see the view to better advantage. We reached home at five. I picked up a white stone with several crystals on it, which I brought home for Morton. In the evening we walked over the farm and went down to see a little calf. A pretty little black thing, of a week old. After tea Louisa and I sang and Mrs. Storrs brought L. some buttermilk

as she had heard her say that she liked it, and I saw her drink it so much as if she liked it that I was tempted to take some too, and to my astonishment & their amusement I found it quite sour and not at all nice.

July 14   I forgot last night to mention the extraordinarily beautiful sunset. There was a heavy cloud resting on the mountain range. As we went up to the Parsonage, a red gleam broke through it, which finally widened into a perfect parallelogram of light, with a few distant golden clouds so arranged as to look like a landscape painted in the sky with the sun's own golden rays. And the framework of heavy clouds around were tinged with colours so as to produce a most novel affect. The sunrise this morning was nearly equally beautiful tho' not so similar. This morning, about twelve, we started for Mr. Prescott's in accordance with Mr. P's invitation. We had a very pleasant call and Louisa and I rec'd permission to go out and see the garden. We found Mr. Prescott there and he showed us all over it, and gave us each a superb bunch of roses of all shades from dark crimson to pure white. And then took us to the orchard where he gave us some delicious cherries, which we declared were too pretty to eat and put with our roses to keep for Uncle Morton, who is passionately fond of flowers and likes cherries better than any other fruit. In the afternoon we went to Beech Hill, going by Cornwallis Bridge to Wolfville and then to Kentville where we left Mrs. Storrs to shop and went up the hill. The view was finer than the last time I was there as the tide was in and it added very much to the beauty of the scene. I got some tissue paper to keep the roses from opening any further before Uncle Morton comes tomorrow.

July 15   Louisa and I were so alarmed at the threatening appearance of the clouds last night, for fear it would rain and Uncle Morton not be able to come for us that we were up at four. For if it rained we should have to take the coach which leaves Kentville at six, as we rec'd letters last night requesting Louisa at least to go to Halifax on Monday. It looked very alarming to us who were not particularity weather wise and could only see the black clouds but Uncle Storrs assured us there was no danger. At about eight o'clock the sun came out brightly. I sewed and Louisa copied music until about eleven, when Uncle Storrs asked us if we would like to go down and see the church, as we could not stay over Sunday for which we are the more sorry, as it is Communion

Sunday and I have not taken the Sacrament since I left Halifax. We went down to Uncle S's tenants to get the key and then went into the church. After going all over it, Uncle S. took us up into the belfry. He was able to go higher than we with our drapery felt equal to, and consequently had a finer view than we could command, but ours amply paid us for the trouble we had in ascending. Louisa felt quite giddy. I did not but my head ached dreadfully with the heat. When we went home I took impression of leaves and Louisa read. After I was tired of the leaves, I mended my gloves and began to work a little on my collar, stationing myself at a window which commanded the furthest view of the road to Wolfville, for it was later than we expected Uncle Morton to come. At last, nearly two o'clock, I saw a straw hat and a horse's head, which as it approached, proved to be Uncle Morton at which I was heartily glad. As we had waited dinner for him and I was very hungry, besides tired, I had felt strongly tempted to lie down for a while after returning from the church, but I was afraid it would make me feel stupid when Uncle Morton came, so I refrained. After dinner, we went and saw that everything was quite ready, showed Uncle M. the roses which he thought had a Chinese appearance in their night caps, as he called them. I gave him a beautiful blush rose to put in his button hole and he wore it, though afterwards faded, the whole day. Uncle Storrs gave me a very pretty book when I came away to remember him by, called "A Life in Earnest." We started about four, bringing the roses and cherries which we ate on the way. I drove the greater part of the way. Coming up the Mt., Uncle M. and Louisa got out and walked for some distance, so to relieve the horse, she to rest herself, as she was tired sitting so long in one position. I sat in front with Uncle Morton as she did on our way to Cornwallis and the back seat is very narrow and consequently not so comfortable as the other. We came by the Mt. Denson road, a very beautiful one, so that I have now been [on] all three of the roads between Windsor & Cornwallis. The first view of the Windsor River and the little villages on the shore is exceedingly lovely. Hansport is the prettiest settlement I have seen. There were three pretty large ships anchored there. A little bit of road, just before we reached the Half Way River, is the prettiest thing I ever remember seeing. My eyes ached very much and were very much inflamed from driving so much and straining to see so much lately. I begged Uncle M. to come to Boston with me, but I do not think he will. Mr. Porter was at the office door watching for us and Harriet King & Mrs. McKay had come to Mrs. Wilkins to take tea with us. Mrs. W. asked Uncle M. to come to tea, but he did not come until quite about nine. He stayed until half-past eleven. He escorted Mrs. McKay home, a little after twelve and we had music, conversation & cake until he went home. He showed me the rose in his button hole when he came in. Aunt Eliza gave him a beautiful bunch of flowers, so he had plenty of them. Fanny Young is here on a visit to Sady. She is a nice little girl, an orphan. Mrs. W. is not going to Halifax on Monday. I do not know whether I shall or not.

July 16   5th Sunday after Trinity. Windsor is so much hotter than Cornwallis. Mrs. McKay sent us in her carriage to church & sent it for us to come home in. I do not know what I should have done if I had had to walk. It is so far in the morning. Mrs. W. was not well and did not go. I did sleep so delightfully last night. My eyes were so painful it was a pleasure to shut them. I woke up half past six, looked at the watch and went to sleep again. Dreamed that I was at home & that they had moved to Mrs. Carter's house and was waked by Aunt Eliza's voice talking to Louisa that it was nine o'clock. We jumped up in a great hurry & so refreshed by our sleep. My eyes are not yet well, but much better. Mr. Gilpin gave a very long sermon this afternoon and it was so intensely hot, that we did not know what to do. When we came home we were sitting up stairs talking when a knock came to the door and I went down, and an old woman of about ninety years old came in. I sat talking with her some time and then came up to ask Mrs. W. to go down and see her, but when she went down stairs Mrs. DesBarres was gone. Mrs. W. says she is an aunt of Judge DesBarres and educated him.[9] I thought she was crazy. I can hardly believe that I am going tomorrow with L. to Halifax. I would give anything I possessed to stay longer, but Mrs. W. seems to take it for granted that we go together, and I cannot help myself so we went down to bid Mrs. McKay good bye. She was very kind and sent her remembrance to Josey.

July 17   Rose at half past five. Aunt Eliza came down early and packed my trunks for me. I felt very sad about going without seeing the academy. At about nine o'clock Dr. Fraser came and said that if only one were going Mrs. Fraser would be happy to offer a seat in her coach. So as Louisa was obliged to go, Mrs. Wilkins said I had better stay a few days to allow L. to take advantage of the offer. I was only too happy. Uncle M. sent me word that he would not go to the academy so I got some purse silk and began to make a watch guard for him. He came in at dinner time and said he liked the guard, and would try to go to the academy tomorrow. He does not look at all well. He came down to see about the coach for us and walked up to Gerrish Hall with Louisa & Aunt Eliza.

July 18 Mr. Porter passed very often today. I was sitting at the window in the morning & Dr. Fraser passed and said he was engaged to dine with Mrs. McKay, and very soon after there came an invitation for Aunt Eliza & me. We had hardly got down there before it poured rain so that again Uncle M. could not take me to the academy. Dr. F. came into the parlor where I was sitting alone and called me Charlotte & kept it up all the rest of the day. Mrs. McKay calls me Griselda always. We had a very pleasant evening. Mrs. McKay gave me a keepsake. After the rain stopped, at Mrs. McKay's request, I went over to the office to ask Uncle M. & Mr. Porter over to tea. Uncle M. was not there & Mr. P. said he was not at all well and he himself could not come either which I thought very shabby for I told him he would never see me again. Mr. Maturin came to Windsor today.

July 19 Uncle M. came to ask me to go to the academy and Judge Haliburton (Sam Slick) made him stay on some disagreeable business but Mrs. McKay took me. Sarah King went with us. The Academy was shut & the housekeeper up at the college, so we drove up to the college, where we found Dr. McCawley who hunted up the housekeeper and sent her down. We drove on a little further and then went to the Academy. The housekeeper was very civil and so was the steward. I went into every room and closet up stairs and down stairs. I was shocked to find the room in which I was born full of masons at their supper. What desecration! I brought away some leaves of a willow overhanging the front door. I stayed to tea with Mrs. McKay & she came up and spent the evening with us. I forgot to say yesterday Dr. F. offered me a seat in his carriage to Halifax as he was going to drive down at two this morning to go to Capt. Gore's wedding and the only reason I did not accept was that I had not seen the Academy.

Return
to
Halifax

Halifax *Part 2*

July 20 Halifax. Uncle M. came down and took my seat in the coach for me and gave me about eight pounds. Mrs. McKay sent Maynard up with a quill box & a pr. of moccasins for me to choose from for another keepsake. I took the box. Mrs. Wilkins gave me a birch bark card-case, her own work. Mr. Maturin was in the coach & I was put in his care. I found him wondering if the Rev. Mr. Clinch was in the coach, seeing a basket with his name upon it. We reached Halifax between five and six. C. Almon came in the evening. I found Louisa and Charlotte still here, as the packet will not go until Saturday. Mrs. Balfour was here when L. reached home last Monday.

July 21 I feel a little tired today. It is not as pleasant travelling in the coach as with Uncle Morton. I went down town this morning with Aunt Mary and Louisa. I got a clasp for the watch guard for Uncle Morton and some lace for Aunt Eliza. I went down again in the afternoon to have the clasp fastened on, and wrote home and took the letter to Mrs. O'Brien. When I came yesterday I found a letter from home awaiting me. Aunt Mary says I can go to Falkland on Sunday with Uncle William, as I was not able to go before I went to Windsor. I wrote to Mrs. Wilkins, Mrs. McKay, Aunt Eliza and Uncle Morton. Dr. Grigor, Emily Wainwright & Miss Stephens came up for Bella is to go down & practice and it came on to rain very heavily.

July 22 I finished a collar I was working. Mrs. & Miss Walford and Mrs. Forbes called on me yesterday. Today Judge & Mrs. & Miss Robie, Mr. Balfour called, having heard that Uncle W. was sick. To my horror, Uncle W. asked him to go to Falkland tomorrow. I though it would put an end to my going and that consequently I should not be able to see it at all but Uncle said that it would make no difference. So I am going, but I feel rather awkward about it.

July 23 I went to St. Luke's this morning. Uncle W. preached. Mr. Morris assisted him to read. At about two I got ready and had just gone down to the parlor to ask something about my veil, when Mr. Balfour came in without ringing. He looked a little surprised when he found I was going, but did not seem to care. Uncle W. & he were talking about the college the greater part of the way until we reached the battery, so I spoke but very little, but when we reached the battery, Uncle W. began to speak of churches and the architecture, and appealed to me for the style of the American churches and when he went on to speak to the ferry man, Mr. B. went on talking to me. He took my prayer book when I got into the boat and kept it until we went into church. I had picked a bit of spruce coming down & held it in my hand. Going over, I said it was the first time I had been in a boat since I had left home & how keenly I enjoyed it. When we landed, we found a very steep, rocky path before us and Halifax behind us made a very pretty view, after we had gone up some way I picked two or three flowers on the way and Mr. B. perceiving it, found a rose and gave it to me. The church is a very pretty one indeed, and the congregation most serious and attentive. I enjoyed the service very much, the cool fresh sea-breeze blowing in, feeling so different from the hot crowded church in the city. The church has a commanding view out to sea, but not so much towards Halifax. Its proportions are beautifully correct and tho' a miniature of a church, it is so small, it looks as if is would be spoiled by being a foot longer. After church we went up to York Redoubt, passing the R.C. chapel on the way. It is a perfect room, the walls inside not being even white washed and tho' the situation is better than ours, it is very faulty & ugly in its architectural proportions. An unusual feeling among the [indecipherable]. To my great joy, they were signaling when we reached the Redoubt. I have always wished to see it closely. Mr. B. showed me the Citadel answering through the telescope which tho' is small is a very excellent one, as are all used there. Halifax looked very pretty being in the shade of Citadel Hill, and Dartmouth opposite, being in brilliant sunlight. St. George's Island looked very pretty, tho' Mr. B says there are nearly one hundred guns there. They are going to practice there tomorrow & Mr. B. asked me if I would like to go. But I was not sure whether he was in earnest or not, or if Ladies went there, even so I laughed it off, and said I should be declining. He showed me many pretty views, and the prettiest point of view of the little church. As we were returning an old man gave us some verses. Uncle W. showed me the mackerel nets all in readiness of tomorrow and explained how they caught the mackerel, [indecipherable] there he said. So when we reached shore we had to walk along a stone walled wharf to the landing place and a net hung there was in the way & I got inside and walked but soon was brought to a stop by finding myself completely trapped. The net was fastened to a wall preventing my advance. Mr. Balfour laughed as he extricated me, and told me I was "like the mackerel circumvented." We had such a pleasant row. When we landed, we saw Mr. Haye walking with Mr. Stoddard & Addie Gore. We had a very pleasant walk home, but Uncle W. was too tired to go to church in the evening and it was so late that he would have been obliged to go without any tea. Miry & Louisa Bliss were just starting so Mr. Balfour walked on with them, went to church (without having dined) & came home with them. I was writing this when he came in. I always happen to be writing something or other when he comes in. He was very much afraid I would be tired, and so I was but he had more reason to be.

July 24   More tired than yesterday. I always am more tired the next day. Miss Morrisey came. It was very warm. I sewed until nearly five and then went down to call upon Miss McKie. She asked me to come down tomorrow and take a lesson and gave me an invitation from Mr. Hartshorne to go to Dartmouth tomorrow. Mr. Balfour took the boys to the Island today to see the firing. When I came home I found Andy Uniacke and Lewis Bliss, who had called upon me. Andy declared his wish to be enrolled in the train of my admirers. The boys came home in high spirits and in love with Mr. Balfour, who had lent them his glass & explained everything to them. There was some very good firing. One man had the target at a distance of 1500 yards. I am very tired. I began another collar, traced about half of it.

July 25   I went down to choir this morning at nine and staid until twelve. It was an unusually warm day and to tantalize me I was drawing boys sliding on the ice. When I came home Miry was writing Charlotte a long account of my Sunday excursion. I was dressing my hair when Charley came running up stairs to say that Mr. Balfour was down stairs & wanted to see me to ask me to go over to the island, as they were shooting again. How angry I was that I had to go to the Hartshorne's, but I finished dressing & went down. He was very sorry, but hoped that before I went home that there would be another opportunity. He thought that on Friday they might be practicing again and if they did, it would be with shells which are far prettier. It was very kind of him, for on Sunday I had told him how soon I was going home, and that I had had no boating and had never seen the island. Miry immediately put a raving postscript to her letter to Charlotte declaring her jealousy and rage &c. laughing all the while so that she could hardly write. We went to Dartmouth, calling upon Mr. McCallum on the way. On the ferry boat we found Major Dennis, Newton Fairbanks & Mr. Boggs. It began to rain before we crossed & as we went to the Fairbanks' to tea, as it was close to the ferry and Mr. Hartshorne's over a mile and a half away. We came away about half past seven. We did not like to stay later as we had no gentlemen with us. Lewis Bliss was in to spend the evening. I hope Friday will be fine. I am very tired.

July 26 I did not rise very early, as I did not feel very well. Went down to draw at nine, but did very little, and at ten felt so dizzy and ill that I gave up and came home. Laid on the sofa for an hour or two and felt better. Worked a very little on my collar. Callers R. Haliburton, L. Bliss, Mary Bliss & Mrs. Odell. We had to go to the Silvers, much to my regret, as I wanted to go to church & did not feel well enough to talk & laugh at a party. I wore my argentine, Bella her white, & Miriam black. I never saw M. look so pretty. Mr. Young, flag lieutenant was there, and made himself very agreeable. If it had not been for him it would have been dreadfully stupid. I though we would never get home. There were some Cambridge girls there. Not very nice.

July 27 I began a letter home today. The *Kingston* is so very long coming in. While I was writing Bella called us that there was a note for me, and I went down and found C. Almon, who was the bearer of an invitation to us from his mother to go out and to row on the Arm. We accepted, and I was so glad it was today instead of tomorrow. I took a nice bath before dressing and enjoyed it very much. There were a number of callers today. I do not know who they all were. But just after a set had gone away I was trying a very dashing Italian song, when in the middle of an unusually high note, there came such a peal at the back, as if who ever it was, was afraid of not being heard in the din. I flew to my workbox and sat down quietly. It was the Lord Bishop. He asked who was singing and said he heard me at the corner of the street. Mr. Balfour came just after the Bishop had gone to tell me that the practicing would take place tomorrow, and a boat would be at my service at any time from 3 1/4 til 6. He hoped 3 1/4 would not be too early. Not at all

I assured him. Uncle W., Aunt M. and Miry & Bella are going besides. I am perfectly delighted and we are going to row on the Arm this evening unless it rains. At present it looks very threatening indeed. Mr. Stinnage called and dined with us today.

We went to Mrs. Almon's and met Mather on the way, but just as we reached the house it began to pour and finding that a row was out of the question, we took off our bonnets and had a delightful evening. The assembled party consisted, besides the Almons, Miss Grove, Miss Anne & Helen Grove, Aunt Mary, Miriam, Bella, Tory, Katy Stewart & me., Uncle W., Mr. Halliburton, Mr. Pearsce, Mr. Walker. I think that was all. The rain stopped after tea, but there being no moon, the night was too dark for a row, so we went out and had a pleasant swing. Mather & Charlie came with us about one o'clock.

June [sic] 28th   The finest morning we have had this summer. I am very glad for if it continues fine, we shall go to the Island today. It is cooler also than any day since I came to Halifax. Uncle W. could not go with us today, so we asked C. Almon to go with us, as we did not like to go to the Engineers Yard without a gentleman. Bella was a little late, and when we reached the yard, they had just given us up and had started. They were not however, more than a couple of yards from the wharf, and returned. We were only two minutes late, but Col. Fraser is very punctual. Besides the rowers there were Col. Fraser, Dr. D'Ausseauville, Mr. Walker, Mr. Balfour, C. Almon. Aunt Mary, Miry, Bella & I were the ladies and when we reached the land found ourselves the only ones, but it was just as pleasant. I did enjoy the day very very much. Mr. Balfour took us to see the guns loaded and fired. The round we stood above the guns. He also took us into the fort, opened the magazines, showed & explained to us shells, different kinds of cannons and methods of shooting, firing &c. The shell practice was exceedingly beautiful. Col. Fraser made Mr. Balfour fire one gun & he did not want to a bit. It was a brilliantly clear day and pleasant cool breeze, while the Citadel was gay with an unusual number of flags, and the harbor fairly studded with shipping of every description, from steamers and merchant men, down to ferry and the smallest description of low-boats. The firing was remarkably good and every one remarkably pleasant & obliging. It was a day to be remembered in my memories of Halifax. Coming home, Miriam went round to see Mr. Walker and brought home an exquisite bunch of flowers. C. Almon spent

"Lobster spearing North West Arm,
Halifax, Nova Scotia"

the evening here, Miriam, Tory, and Katy went one to the Stephens' for an hour or two. I escaped on plea of fatigue. Uncle W. had a letter from father today. All are well except Beppo, who suffers still from his teeth. I rec'd a note from Aunt Eliza with a parcel I left in Windsor.

July 30 Yesterday Bella and I were sick in bed all day and today being damp we could not go to church. Indeed we did not get up until nearly two o'clock. It is the first time I have not been to church on Sunday, at least twice since I came to Halifax, and for us long before I can recollect except while I was sick last summer. I hope it may be as long again before I am away from church. I do not feel very well today, but still better than yesterday. Uncle William has a head ache coming on.

July 31 Bella and I very fashionably took our break-fast in bed, and rose about ten, feeling a great inclination to lie down and rest constantly which rendered dressing rather a long operation. A day with such beginnings would hardly be a very industrious one, so we spent it in, reading a little, working a little, practicing a little & lying down a little. There were several visitors most of whom I escaped by being upstairs. There was a false alarm that the steamer was coming in and C. & H. Almon came down to know if I would go in her. In the afternoon, or rather just at sun-set, a real signal came for it. I was very glad that I had made up my mind not to go in her, for besides my feeling ill and weak, it came so much sooner than it was expected, that I should have missed several things that I wished to see, such as the Garrison Chapel & Donavan's &c. But just as I had finished my tea, and the others were finishing, a ring came and Miriam, who went up to receive whoever it might be, called me & after a pause, Aunt Mary & the others. Aunt M. said she had seen some one in the street who looked like Morton & without waiting to hear more I went up stairs as fast as I could. Mr. Balfour was up there, having called he said to bid me good-bye, and as he was going to the steamer to see a brother officer (Capt. Beddingfield) off, he had hoped to accompany me so far. I don't know that he quite liked being fooled into a visit and wasting his sympathy for nothing but for all that he made a long and pleasant call. At nine o'clock he had to go for fear of missing Capt. Beddingfield who has been ordered to Montreal. He left Squib here at Bella's request but Squib made off on the first opportunity. I told Mr. Balfour that

I should certainly go in the next boat. It is a most delightful evening.

August 1 ✑ I rose early today and breakfasted with the others. Worked a little, and went down town to shop. I am going home so soon that I wish to put together a few things to take with me. It is the first time I have been out of doors since Friday. I came home rather tired, but well pleased with my success, as I obtained almost everything I wanted. The fleas have been terrible today. I did not sleep a moment last night until about an hour after the morning gun fired. Lewis Bliss & C. Almon spent the evening here.

August 2 ✑ Was kept awake nearly all night and was late down this morning. It was very damp and foggy and at one time rained and blew quite violently. I spent the morning darning stockings and untrimming my bonnet and working on my collar. I was very anxious to go to church this evening, but it was so very dark that I was afraid. Besides Mr. & Mrs. Shreve & Mr. Boggs were coming up to tea. Before the arrival of either, we had to welcome a very unexpected guest, Heber. We did not think at the earliest he would be here before tomorrow. Mr. Ward in Yarmouth told him that we live opposite the blind asylum. I suppose it is Mr. Monk's house after all. Heber brought a note from Aunt Eliza.

Aug. 3 ✑ The coolest morning since I returned fr. Windsor, the thermometer standing at 60°. I spent the morning in trimming my dark bonnet and arranging Heber's books which were in disorder. Worked upon my collar, saw visitors, among others the Misses Grove, who brought up the English papers. We went to a very dull party at Mrs. Payne Jilous' and when we came home found C. Almon and Gus Allison up here waiting for the steamer as Mr. & Mrs. C. Allison are expected. They are here still but I am tired and have gone to bed.

Aug. 4 ✑ It was very warm indeed this morning and Miry & I felt excessively dull and tired after that heavy party last night. This afternoon Aunt Mary went with me to call on Mrs. & Dr. Twining to ask her to take me to the Garrison Chapel next Sunday which she readily promised to do. We had a very pleasant call and then went on to the gardens. I felt a little tired coming home. We found Mary Bliss at home. She said that all were going to Mr. A. Uniacke's to dinner except Louisa who wanted Miry and me to go over and take tea with her. That is the kind of going out I like. We have had such a pleasant evening. The greater part of the time in the garden which is looking really beautiful. Heber came for us, and when we came home, we found M. Balfour here. He had been spending the evening here. He stayed nearly an hour after we came home and then went away. He is very pleasant indeed. The steamer from England brought the (to us) sad news that Dr. Munro was actually ordered off to the war, appointed to the 93rd Highland Regiment. We are so very sorry.

August 5 ≈ᶾ Rose rather early but very tired. Sewed a good deal and practiced a little. I finished the collar I was making, all but binding it. Heber went out boating and bathing with the boys this morning and brought home between forty & fifty mackerel. He went out in the boat again with Mr. Balfour. Rec'd an invitation to Mrs. Grove's for Monday evening and to McNab's Island for a picnic Wednesday. The Sunday school picnic is on Tuesday. I do not think I shall go. Mr. Harris came to ask Heber to be his groomsman.

August 6 ≈ᶾ It was very warm this morning. At half past ten I went to Dr. Twining's and found him all ready for me. The walk was very warm indeed, but the church was as cool as possible. I like Dr. Twining better than I expected, but that is not saying much. The church itself is large, pleasant, and airy but reminds me too much of the Half Way House, with its blue walls Apicked out as Mr. Balfour says, with white. There were more civilians there than I expected to find. Bella went to Falkland with Heber today. I shall go again if I can before I leave Halifax. One thing appeared strange in the Garrison Chapel this morning was that the clerk gave out the Psalm and Hymn. I had never heard it before. This afternoon St. Luke's felt very warm after the chapel but I like it better. It seems to me more church-like than the chapel, full of uniforms and guilt and glitter. I went to church this evening and heard Mr. DeBlois preach a very lackadaisical sermon indeed. It was such a glorious night when we came home that we stayed about an hour in the garden. Judge Bliss gave me a superb carnation this afternoon and I took it to church with me this afternoon.

Aug. 7 ≈ᶾ I packed up all my winter things today and finished my barege & gingham skirts as far as I could, in expectation of Miss Morrisey & bound the collar I finished. Saturday called upon Mrs. C. Allison, (Bessie Rand), Mrs. T. Twining, Bessie Boggs, and Mrs. Pryor. Mrs. Pryor told me that the *Halifax*, which was aground on Cape Sable, got off, and I may get letters tomorrow. It was Heber's first day of school. He had twelve boys. We spent the evening at Miss Grove's. We met Mather Allison going down and he turned and walked down with us. We had a pleasant evening, but my head ached very much. The moon is at the full, and the night glorious. Lilly Allison asked Miry to be a bridesmaid. Heber to be groomsman, a fortnight from tomorrow.

Aug. 8 Miss Morrisey came today to make Aunt Mary's dress and is coming on Monday to make mine. Aunt M. and I staid home to sew, the others went to the Sunday School picnic. I should have been glad to go, but I must go to McNab's Island tomorrow and should be tired out. They all enjoyed it very much but are very tired. Mr Balfour went, although he was suffering very much from a tooth ache, or something of that kind. Last night Miry and I were alarmed by some noise or other, & roused Heber and we had no more sleep after that, unrefreshed. Heber told Mr. Balfour of it and he laughed at us well for being alarmed easily. In the evening Aunt Mary, Fred, & I went out for a walk and went nearly to Oaklands. The *Halifax* is in but I can not have my letters until morning. It is very late, for the party from Oaklands, did not come home until twelve o'clock perfectly fagged out. I have been reading *The New Times*.

August 9 From being so tired yesterday, we did not get up in very good spirits for the picnic today. Aunt Mary, Miry, Tory, and I went to church and a little after went down to Mr. McNab's. We found a large party assembled there. Mr. McNab introduced a Mr. Tanvurin to me, whom I lost sight of afterwards as he had to go in a different boat from me. Miry went in Mat Almon's boat and Bella & I in Dr. Grigor's. Our party was one of the best I think and I enjoyed it very much but at the island it was very tiresome. It is very pretty but there were very few there whom I knew very well or cared to know. Coming home we were becalmed and had to row in boats the greater part of the way. I liked it far better but I fancied the gentlemen found it rather hard work. It was a terrible bore to go to the party in the evening, as everyone was almost tired out. I was completely. We came home about twelve. I have rec'd a letter from Mother, she had not received mine by the steamer.

Augusta Haliburton with her husband, ca 1865

Augusta Haliburton picnicking with her husband Alexander and an unknown woman,
circa 1865. Augusta was the second daughter
of T.C. and Louisa Haliburton.

Aug. 10   Wrote to Uncle Morton and Aunt Eliza. I was so stiff when I arose this morning that I did not know what to do. This afternoon, tho very tired, I had to go up to Dutch Town to make some calls and get my passage in the steamer which I accomplished under the name Miss Finch as the man had written it. Uncle William compassionate to my fatigue, tho I declared I should walk, insisted upon riding up from the Province Building to the Dock Yard. We called at Mr. Clarke's, Mrs. Fitz-Uniacke, Mrs. Cunard, & Mr. Boggs. Then I shopped & got several things I wanted, and priced a portmanteau which I longed for, but it was too high. I was afraid of not being able to carry home some things I wished to. I am very tired. Miss Fraser called this morning & gave me a parcel to give to Mother. Heber & Miry went to Dartmouth to tea.

Sally went down town, to get a shower bath but she did not like it much, for when it rained hard, she shrugged up her shoulders so, & shut her eyes. It made me laugh in the street.

She has been very good since she had been here, only a little bit too extravagant. She is also very susceptible, having fallen in love with the same young gentleman many times ——- Tory.

Stars teach as well as shine!!!!

Tory.-

(See preceding page)[1]

Aug. 11   Intended to go down town today, as Mrs. Clarke had offered her carriage, but it rained so we could not go. I went down town however as I was obliged to get some things for Miss Morrisey, but I fear I shall be disappointed, as she is sick today. I hope she will be well before Monday. I really do not know what I shall do if she does not come. This morning, while I was dressing, Aunt Mary came up and laid on the toilet the portmanteau I wanted yesterday as a present from Uncle William. It is a very pretty one indeed. I wrote to mother today, as the *Africa* goes tomorrow.

Aug. 12 Perked up a little, and sewed on my dress to be ready as far as possible for Miss Morrisey. Began a black silk apron. Mrs. Clarke did not send her carriage today either, so we went to make some fare well calls. Made eleven and came home tired out. Mr. Balfour called while we were gone. This evening I went into the school room to help Fred with his Latin and when I came into the parlor again, found a hansom card case lying on my work box as a present from Aunt Mary and my cousins. Capt. & Mrs. Gore called today.

Aug. 13 I intended to go to Falkland today but the weather looked so uncertain that Aunt Mary thought I had better not. Cousin Ben came back to Halifax today and came up to see me and announced his arrival. Went down to church this evening where Heber was laid violent hands, or rather tongues, upon by a Mrs. Barry for not being to see her as he had promised. Mr. Balfour sat in the seat with us. Heber preached. I was glad to hear him once before I left. The Bishop walked up with the Blisses & visited.

Postscript

Sarah's diary ends here rather abruptly. She probably obtained passage on a steamer unexpectedly and had to prepare quickly for her voyage, leaving her diary an unfinished memento of her trip.

Little is known of Sarah's life following her return to Boston. Six years following her visit to Nova Scotia the American Civil War began. While the fighting never reached Boston, Sarah no doubt felt its impact—human loss strangely matched by an economic boom for the industrial port city of Boston. In the years preceding the war, Boston had become a center for the abolitionist movement with its own branch of the American Anti-Slavery Society, driven by Bostonians like William Garrison.

On November 25, 1858, Sarah married Richard Fitfield Bond, a member of a well-to-do family and an old friend and suitor. (The same suitor who proposed to Sarah while she was in Halifax.) Following his father's death in 1859, Richard continued the family clock- and watch-making business, and became a well-known and respected Boston craftsman. The couple had three children: William Cranch, born Christmas Day, 1860; Edith Griselda, born May 29, 1862; and Mary Wentworth, born August 26, 1863. Sadly, Sarah was widowed in 1866 at the age of thirty-one with three children under the age of six to care for. She had complained mildly of Richard's "delicate health" in her diary, and it was perhaps this ill health that brought his untimely death. Tragedy struck again in 1871 when Sarah's youngest brother, Beppo (Joseph Howard), died at the age of eighteen.

Throughout her life, Sarah remained close to her Nova Scotian relatives. The collection of the Massachusetts Historical Society includes correspondence to Sarah from her cousins in Halifax, written to console her on the death of her mother Griselda in 1873. Sarah and her mother were very close, and Sarah would have been devastated by the loss.

In 1858 William Bullock was appointed the first rector of St. Luke's Church by Bishop Binney. This was particularly significant as three years later, in 1861, the bishop made the controversial decision to remove cathedral status from St. Paul's and give it to St.

Luke's, formerly known as a "chapel of ease." William died on March 10, 1874. Mary Bullock died January 2,1885. The pain of these deaths was communicated by letter from Sarah's cousins.

Sarah's uncle Perez Morton Cunningham died in 1866 of "atrophy of [the] liver." Following his death, the estate was sold to Samuel Starr.[1]

Interestingly, Morton's close friend and business partner Reginald Porter died five days later of "chronic disease of [the] stomach." Reginald's name even followed Morton's in the provincial death registry. The pair had lived together until the early 1860s when they each built their own home in Windsor. Morton built his on the corner of Wiley and Albert streets and Reginald, whose home became known as Elmcroft, built his on Albert Street. Court of Probate documents related to Morton's estate record that he willed all of his belongings to his sister Eliza, Reginald, and a friend, Edward Dimock. Curiously, the records also note that Morton had a wife named Fanny. Nothing was left to Fanny; in fact, she is never mentioned by Sarah in her diary, nor is there a church or civil record of the marriage. (This is unusual considering the family's strong ties to the Church of England.) Presumably, the couple was married after 1854, as Sarah never mentions Fanny and acknowledges that her uncle is a bachelor. Perhaps Morton married late in life, looking to leave a male heir to the Cunningham estate. Because Reginald died so soon after Morton, the estate was divided between Eliza and Edward.

Upon hearing of Morton's and Reginald's deaths, Rev. E.E.B. Nichols, an acquaintance, recorded the following in his diary: "Last week heard of the sudden death of P.M. Cunningham and today of that of his friend Porter. How many scenes of youthful sin and folly do their names recall – How far their example gave an

Reverend Heber Bullock, ca. 1870

impetus to the downward & indecency of many a once promising collegian. God alone can tell. I trust they had grace given them to prepare for this last great charge!"

Sarah and her family were no doubt saddened by the death of Morton. It is clear from her diaries that Sarah was very fond of her uncle. While to the modern reader, Morton and Reginald's relationship might appear to go beyond that of friendship, Sarah's diary does not reveal the exact nature of that relationship and so it cannot be known. As is clear from Sarah's diary, the community knew of the close friendship between the men; Reginald was normally extended an invitation to join Morton at dinner parties and other gatherings. Regardless of the nature of their relationship, both had busy careers in law. Morton held several government appointments and could count some of Nova Scotia's most influential men as his acquaintances, if not his friends.

Sarah's cousin Heber Bullock continued a long and prestigious career in the Church of England. In 1855 he was appointed chaplain to the British forces. This position took him all over the world, including a station in Malta, where he remained for twelve years. He retired from active service in 1888 and returned to Halifax. In 1898 Heber was made Queen's Honorary Chaplain and in 1905 was appointed Honorary Canon of All Saints Cathedral. The Diocesan Yearbook described him as a man of strong faith, a nature lover, an expressive writer, a lover of good, and a man respected by all who knew him. Heber died September 26, 1917.

It seems that Sarah never remarried following the premature death of her husband. She continued to live in South Boston on Quincy Street. Correspondence between Sarah and her Canadian cousins reveals that she played a large role in the Bond family business, as did her brother Morton. Sarah also owned several houses close to Harvard University, and rented rooms to students. While it is doubtful she inherited much from her father's estate, as the daughter of a Church of England clergyman she was entitled to a somewhat generous annual stipend from the "Society for the Relief of the Widows and Orhpans of Deceased Clergymen of the Protestant Episcopal Church." With support from the Bond family, income from her role in the family business, and her real estate interests, Sarah probably managed to continue to live her upper middle-class lifestyle despite occasional setbacks. Sarah and her Canadian cousins continued to be close, corresponding and visiting throughout her life. Sarah died circa 1900 in Boston.

Endnotes

Boston

1   Reference to Dr. James and Mary Farish of Yarmouth, Nova Scotia. James was the son of Dr. Henry Greggs Farish and Mary was the daughter of Rev. William and Mary Bullock, and Sarah's cousin. The couple lived in Yarmouth where James continued his father's medical practice.
2   Wendell Phillips was a Boston abolitionist and political reformer. He was well known for his eloquent anti-slavery public speeches.
3   A whitlow refers to any inflammation of the finger or toe nail.
4   *Stanley Sadie's Music Guide, An Introduction*, Stanley Sadie and Alison Latham eds.
5   A reference to a piece of music composed by Gottschalk, "Grande Fantaisie triomphale sur l'hymne national brésilien."
6   Jullien Fontana, a peer of Gottschalk and a renowned conductor.

Halifax

1   The Haliburton's first child, Susannah, was born in 1817; she married John Weldon and moved to Annapolis Royal. William Neville was born in 1819 and died in childhood. Twins Thomas and Lewis, born in 1821, also died young. Augusta was born in 1823 and married her English cousin Alexander Fowden Haliburton during Sarah's stay. Laura, born in 1824, married William Cunard, the son of Sir Samuel Cunard. William Frederick was born in 1826 and died a year later. Emma was born in 1828; an amateur artist, she married Rev. John Bainbridge Smith. Amelia was born in 1829 and married Rev. Edwin Gilpin. Robert was born in 1831. Finally, Arthur, born in 1831, married Marianna Clay and became a lawyer.
2   Mrs. Bamble was most likely the Bullock family housekeeper.
3   Sarah Rachel Gore was the wife of Colonel Charles Gore, commander of the British forces at Halifax. The couple had six children. Sarah was the daughter of the Hon. James Fraser, legislative councilor.
4   The Chain Battery was located in Point Pleasant Park on the North West Arm.
5   Eliza Cunningham was the sister of Sarah's mother. Eliza never married and resided in Windsor, Nova Scotia.
6   James Twining was the son of Rev. Dr. John Twining, curate at St. Paul's Church.
7   The letter, clearly romantic in nature, was from Richard Bond, a long-time family friend.
8   Mrs. Binney is probably a reference to Bishop Hibbert Binney's moth-

er, as he was not married until 1855.

9　Rev. George Hill was an Anglican minister. Hill, like Bullock and Clinch, was a graduate of King's College who shared preaching duties with other clergy, including Bullock. He was ordained in 1850; in 1859 he was appointed curate at St. Paul's and in 1865 rector, a position he retained until 1885. He was one of the founders of the Nova Scotia Historical Society and sat on the board of Dalhousie College.

10　Lady Le Marchant's husband was Sir John Gaspard, Governor General of Nova Scotia, 1852-1858.

11　Langley's Store refers to W.M. Langley & Johnson, chemist and druggist, located on Hollis Street, just south of Province House.

12　Sticks of opium used for medicinal purposes.

13　Rev. Harry Leigh Yewens was born in London, England in 1825 to William and Mary Yewens. He came to Nova Scotia as a Society for the Propagation of the Gospel teacher. In 1852 he was ordained deacon, as Sarah described in December 1853. He served as curate to Sarah's uncle John Storrs at Cornwallis until 1855, when he became a missionary in charge of the District of St. James, Kentville. He married Katherine Blake and resided in Kentville. In 1863 he was appointed rector of Trinity Church, which was founded by Rev. William Bullock, Digby. He ended his career at St. John's Church, Franklin, Pennsylvania and died in 1897.

14　Steel's Pond was a large pond located on the lower road which lead into Point Pleasant Park.

15　In Greek mythology, Damocles was a member of the court of Dionysius the Elder and one of his flatterers. Dionysius forced Damocles to sit at a banquet under a sword suspended by a single hair to demonstrate the precariousness of a king's riches.

16　Ellen Rebecca and Elizabeth (Bessie) Rand were the daughters of Caleb Handley and Rebecca Allison Rand. Caleb was a Kentville lawyer and maintained a large home there. When in Kentville, the family attended St. John's Church, Cornwallis. Ellen Rebecca married Mather Byles Almon Jr. and Bessie married her cousin Charles Allison on June 30, 1854.

17　Mrs. J. Allison was Anne Elizabeth Allison, who married the Hon. Joseph Allison.

18　Mr. Charles Thomas Allison married Matilda Elizabeth. Samuel Prescott Fairbanks (1795-1882) was the son of Rufus and Anne Prescott. In 1820 he married Charlotte Ann Newton (granddaughter of Samuel Perkins) Fairbanks and they had several children, including Charlotte and Gus. Samuel Fairbanks attended King's College, Windsor and studied law. He held numerous government appointments, including a controversial period in office as provincial treasurer

19   May he who has earned it take the prize. (Translation by Peter O'Brien.)

20   Mary Bliss was the daughter of Sarah Ann Anderson and William Blowers Bliss. Mary married Bishop Hibbert Binney in 1855.

21   Sarah Rachel Wilkins was the daughter of Nathaniel R. Thomas of Windsor. She married the Hon. Lewis Morris Wilkins, lawyer and MLA. The couple maintained homes in both Halifax and Windsor and had a reputation for being lavish entertainers.

22   Minnie Wilkins was the daughter of the Hon. Lewis Morris and Sarah Wilkins.

23   Reference to William Valentine, a well-known artist and dauguerreo-typist. Born in 1789 in England, he removed to Halifax as an adult, married Susannah Elizabeth and, following her death, married Sarah Ann Selon. Valentine painted portraits of many influential Nova Scotians. Between 125 and 150 of his pieces have survived, despite a fire in his studio several years prior to his death that destroyed many of his portraits and much of his photographic equipment. He died at Halifax in 1849.

24   From Horace's *Satires 3*. This is the vice of all singers: that when they are asked to sing among their friends, they can never bring themselves to do it; when they are uninvited, they never cease. (Translation by Peter O'Brien.)

25   The handwriting of this paragraph is not Sarah's. It is most likely Heber's.

26   Rev. Benjamin Gerrish Gray, D.D was the son of Joseph and Mary Gerrish Gray, born in 1768 at Boston. He married Mary Thomas and they had one son. Gray received his early education in England and later King's College, Windsor. He was ordained deacon in 1796 and priest in 1797. Throughout his life he held various religious and teaching positions ending his career as rector of Trinity Church, Saint John, N.B. He died at Saint John. He was the grandfather of Ben Gray and he married Sarah's grandparents at Prince's Lodge.

27   Sir George Seymour was Admiral of the Fleet and, in 1853, was named Commander-in-Chief of the Atlantic Station.

28   Early in 1854 Morton was appointed one of the commissioners for the construction and management of a proposed railway that was to run between Halifax and Windsor.

29   Todd Thomas Jones taught at a school he operated jointly with his close friend Heber Bullock. According to probate records, he died of "[the] presence of disease of the al[a]rge[d] vessels of the heart." Todd left Heber his library and his share of the furniture they purchased

together. To Louisa Bullock, he left four shares in the Bank of North America. Todd's family lived in England, and for the last few months of his life he lived with the Bullock family.

Windsor & Cornwallis

1 Gwen Shand papers, NSARM. MGI 2384 and 2385.
2 Rev. Edwin Gilpin Jr., son of Rev. Edwin and Eliza Gilpin. He married Amelia MacKay Haliburton, the fifth daughter of Judge Thomas Chandler Haliburton. Edwin Gilpin Jr. became Dean of All Saints Cathedral, Halifax and died at Halifax in 1906.
3 Judge Harry King was a Windsor lawyer and later a probate judge. He was the fourth son of Rev. William Colsell King (friend of Richard Cunningham) and Harriet Sophia DeWolfe. He married Margaret Halliburton and the couple had four daughters, Harriet being the third.
4 This could be Mrs. Tamar Starr, wife of Col. Richard Starr, brother of Samuel Starr. Tamar was born in Bridgetown, where Sarah's father was appointed early in his career as an Anglican priest. Mrs. Starr also lived at Starr's Point and her husband Richard became very good friends with Charles Ramage Prescott.
5 It is curious that Sarah calls him Robert, as this must be Charles Ramage Prescott because later she mentions that Mrs. Prescott's sister—a Miss Hammell—lived in the house. C.R. Prescott married a Maria Hammell. He did have one son James Robert; however, he lived in Kentville and never married.
6 Olivia Barrs was the daughter of Judge Elisha and Margaret DeWolf and married Capt. Joseph Barss. The couple had nine children.
7 Amelia MacKay Gilpin, wife of Rev. Edwin Gilpin and the daughter of Judge Thomas Chandler Haliburton.
8 Judge William Blowers Bliss kept a home in the area because for a time he represented Hants County in the provincial legislature.
9 Billtown, a tiny farming community in King's County, was settled in 1770 by the Bill family.
10 Judge William Frederick DesBarres was a lawyer, M.L.A. and later Supine Judge of the Supreme Court. He studied law with Judge L.M. Wilkins Sr.

Halifax-Part Two

1 The handwriting here is Tory's, not Sarah's. "Sally" was Sarah's nick-name, which she became commonly known by in her adult life.

Postscript

1 Samuel and Susannah Starr had seven children, including two girls: Paulina, born in 1823, and Martha, born in 1836. Martha married Gilbert Fowler. Susannah Starr died in 1852.

List of Illustrations

Front cover: "Four Ladies in Evening Dress," Emma Haliburton, 1840-1846.

Title page: "View of Halifax," unknown artist, ca. 1850.

p.3 "William Cranch Bond," unknown artist, ca. 1840. (Harvard College Observatory Archives)

p.4 "Harvard College Observatory," unknown artist, ca. 1852. (Harvard College Observatory Archives)

p.5 Signal flags. (Courtesy Army Museum Archives)

p.7 "Phrenology Sketch," attributed to Dr. Henry Greggs Farish, ca. 1820. (Courtesy Yarmouth County Museum Archives; Dr. Henry Greggs Farish fonds.)

p.11 Gottschalk concert. Reprinted from *Stanley Sadie's Music Guide, An Introduction*, Stanley Sadie and Alison Latham eds., Prentice Hall, New Jersey, 1987.

p.17 Rev. William Bullock, ca. 1865 (NSARM, Notman Studio Collection,)

p.18 Mary Bullock, ca. 1870 (NSARM, no. 39198, Notman Studio Collection)

p.19 Corner of South and Queen streets, ca. 1870. (NSARM, no. 6880, Royal Engineers Collection)

p.20 Reverend Heber Bullock, ca. 1870 (NSARM, n-3996, Rev. E.E.B. Nichols fonds) p.21 Louisa and Charlotte Bullock, ca. 1870 (NSARM, no. 44899, Notman Studio Collection)

p.23 View of Halifax from Bullock Home, ca. 1870. (NSARM, Royal Engineers Collection)

p.24 William DeBlois, William Chase, ca. 1865. (NSARM, album #5, no. 94)

p.26 Officers of the 76th Regiment, 1871. (Courtesy Army Museum Archives, Citadel Hill)

p.27 "Encampment of Artillery and 76th Regiment at Point Pleasant," Lieutenant-Colonel James Fox Bland, 1855. (Courtesy National Archives of Canada, C-000496)

p.28 Rev. Edward Maturin, Gauvin and Gentzel Studio, 1875. (NSARM)

p.30 "Dr. Wm Grigor," William Valentine, 1838. (Nova Scotia Museum)

p.32 Mrs. Mary Bullock, ca. 1870. (Courtesy Anglican Diocesan Archives)

p.35 "Brevet Major Bland, Captain Tidd and Lacy of the 76th Foot Regiment at the Citadel," ca. 1855 (108-01-2-855-0223)

p.37 Admiralty House, ca. 1865. (NSARM)

p.39 Bishop Hibbert Binney, ca. 1855 (Courtesy Anglican Diocesan Archives)

p.42 Arthur Haliburton, unknown artist, ca. 1873 (Courtesy Acadia University Archives)

p.43 Thomas Chandler Haliburton, ca. 1860. (Courtesy Acadia University Archives)

p.44 Laura Haliburton Cunard, ca. 1880. (Courtesy Acadia University Archives)

p.44 Louisa Neville Haliburton, 1836 (photograph of a portrait by William Valentine. (NSARM)

p.45 Emma Maria Haliburton, ca. 1870. (Courtesy Acadia University Archives)

p.46 St. Paul's Church trimmed for Christmas," ca. 1886-1892 (NSARM, no. 70639, Notman Studio Collection)

p.47 Charles Bullock, ca. 1870 (NSARM, no. 51589, Notman Studio

Collection)

p.48 Interior of St. Luke's Church, ca. 1890 (NSARM)

p.50 St. Paul's Chancel, ca. 1856 (Courtesy Anglican Diocesan Archives)

p.50 Elizabeth Mary Uniacke, ca. 1865 (NSARM album #18, no. 23)

p.52 Fancy Dress Ball, 1883 (Notman Collection, No. 100004, NSARM)

p.58 "Luncheon at the Mess Hall on the Day of the Sham fight," Emma Haliburton, 1844. (Courtesy NAC, Lady Falkland Album, C-003418)

p.59 "Falkland Village," unknown artist, 1846 (Courtesy NAC, Lady Falkland Album, C-105119)

p.62 Royal Artillery Mess, ca. 1870 (Courtesy Army Museum Archives)

p.62 Royal Artillery Park, ca. 1870 (Courtesy Army Museum Archives)

p.64 Silhouette of Elizabeth Gould Franklin, J. Hankers, ca. 1831. (NSARM)

p.65 Rev. Robert Fitz-Uniacke (NSARM, album #18, no. 12)

p.68 "Sledding on Citadel Hill," Lieut.-Colonel James Fox Bland, 1853. Originally published in the *London Illustrated News*. (Courtesy Army Museum Archives)

p.80 Skating Party on the Dartmouth Lakes, ca. 1855 (Dartmouth Heritage Museum, 79.68.1,)

p.81 "English and Newfoundland Mail Vessels in Halifax Harbour," George Henry Andrews, 1861. (Courtesy NAC C-013287)

p.84 Garrison Chapel, 1890. (NSARM, Postcard collection)

p.85 Augusta Neville Haliburton, ca. 1880. (Courtesy Acadia University Archives)

p.87 Martello Tower, Point Pleasant Park, ca. 1870. (NSARM, Notman Studio Collection, no. 1692)

p.90 "Portrait of a woman," Mary R. McKie, 1840-1846. (Courtesy, NAC, Lady Falkland Album, 1990-207-52)

p.91 "Nova Scotian Negro youth," Mary R. McKie, ca. 1840-1846. (Courtesy NAC, Lady Falkland Album, C-009564) p.94 "Man and woman sleighing," William Smyth Maynard Wolfe, 1853-1854 (Courtesy NAC, William Smyth Maynard Wolfe Album, C-122497)

p.108 General C. Gore, ca.1865. (NSARM, Album #7, no. 74)

p.110 Bellevue House, William Chase, ca. 1860. (NSARM, Album #5, no. 55)

p.113 "Point Pleasant Battery," Alexander Cavalié Mercer, 1842 (Courtesy NAC, C-035942)

p.116 "Chocolate Lake from Wood near its Head," Alexander Cavalié Mercer, 1842 (Courtesy NAC, C-013755)

p.117 "Three Mile Church," 1840-1846, unknown artist. (Courtesy NAC, Lady Falkland Album, C-105134)

p.119 Andrew Downs with his two dogs, ca. 1870. (NSARM)

p.124 Engraving of the Collegiate School, ca. 1869, 'A.W.' Reprinted from the Collegiate School Calendar, 1869. (NSARM)

p.125 "Kings College Campus,", 18- (NSARM)

p.126 "Grounds and Summer House at the Duke of Kent's Country Residence near Halifax," William Acland, 1860 (Courtesy National Archives of Canada, C-096910K)

p.128 St. John's Anglican Church, Cornwallis, ca. 1920. (Courtesy Anglican Diocesan Archives)

p.129 "Ten women and four men in evening dress," Emma Haliburton, 1840-1842 (Lady Falkland Album, C-003419, NAC)

p.135 Christ Church, Windsor, ca. 1890 (NSARM)

p.138 Sophia Almon, ca. 1870. (NSARM)

p.139 Rev. Dr. George McCawley, ca. 1870. (Courtesy Anglican Diocese of Nova Scotia Archives)

p.140 Mrs. Anne McCawley, ca. 1870. (Courtesy Anglican Diocese of Nova Scotia Archives)

p.141 Fort Lawrence, Windsor, ca. 1955. (Courtesy Elayne Mott)

p.142 Clifton House, ca. 1890. (NSARM)

p.143 Martock House, ca, 1865. (NSARM)

p.145 View of Windsor from the Residence of Chief Justice Haliburton, Bartlett, 1842 (NSARM) p.160 "Lobster spearing North West Arm." (Courtesy NAC)

p.165 Augusta Haliburton with her husband, ca. 1865. (Courtesy Acadia University Archives)

p.169 Reverend Heber Bullock, ca 1870. (Rev. E.E.B. Nichols fonds, 33.5.2)

Bibliography

Abrahamson, Una. *God Bless Our Home: Domestic Life in Nineteenth-Century Canada*. Burns and MacEachern: Toronto, 1967.

Buebner, Philip A. and John G. Reid, eds. *The Atlantic Region to Confederation: A History*. Acadiensis Press and University of Toronto Press: Fredericton and Toronto, 1994.

Conrad, Margaret, ed. *Intimate Relations: Family and Community in Planter Nova Scotia, 1759-1800*. Acadiensis Press: Fredericton, N.B., 1995.

Conrad, Margaret, Toni Laidlaw and Donna Smyth, eds. *No Place Like Home: Diaries and Letters of Nova Scotia Women, 1771-1938*. Formac: Halifax, N.S., 1988.

Diocesan Yearbook, 1916-1917, NSARM.

Emsley, Sarah Baxter. *St. Paul's in the Grand Parade*. Formac: Halifax, N.S., 1999.

Fingard, Judith, Janet Guildord and David Sutherland. *Halifax, the First Years*. Formac: Halifax, N.S., 1999.

Gwen Shand Papers, NSARM, MG1 Vol. 2384 and 2385.

Harris, Reginald V. *The History of King's Collegiate School, Windsor, N.S.: 1788-1938*. "The Outlook": Middleton, N.S., 1938.

Judith Fingard, *The Dark Side of Life in Victorian Halifax*. Pottersfield Press: Porter's Lake, N.S., 1989.

Millington, Elsie. *Purcell's Cove – The Little Place and Helped Build a City*, 2000.

Milman, Thomas R. and A.R. Kelley. *Atlantic Canada to 1900. A History of the Anglican Church*. Anglican Book Centre:

Toronto, 1983.

Morton Cunningham Clinch Papers, 1754-1903. Massachusetts Historical Society.

Register of Deaths, Hants County, mfm 16524, NSARM.

Rev. E.G.B. Nichols fonds , Vol. 1056, Diary 1846-1868, NSARM

Rossiter, William S. *Days and Ways in Old Boston.* Stearns and Co.: Boston, 1915.

Sadie, Stanley and Alison Latham, eds. *Stanley Sadie's Music Guide, An Introduction.* Prentice Hall: New Jersey, 1987.

Shand, Gwen. "Historic Hants County."

Thomas, C.E. "Rev. William Bullock." *The Nova Scotia Historical Society,* Vol. 37.

Vroom, F.W. "King's College, A Chronicle, 1789-1939."

Index